2 IN 1: POSITIVE AFFIRMATIONS FOR BLACK WOMEN

CULTIVATE AN EMPOWERED MINDSET + OVER 1,000 AFFIRMATIONS TO READ OR LISTEN TO ANYTIME, ANYWHERE

IMANI ELKINS

Copyright © 2024 Akeso Publishing. All rights reserved.

The content within this book may not be reproduced, duplicated, or transmitted in any form or by any electronic or mechanical means, including information storage and retrieval systems without direct written permission from the author or the publisher, except for the use of brief quotations in a book review.

Under no circumstances will any blame or legal responsibility be held against the publisher, or author, for any damages, reparation, or monetary loss due to the information contained within this book, either directly or indirectly.

Legal Notice:

This book is copyright protected. It is only for personal use. You cannot amend, distribute, sell, use, quote, or paraphrase any part of the content within this book without the consent of the author or publisher.

Disclaimer Notice:

Please note the information contained within this document is for educational and entertainment purposes only. All effort has been expended to present accurate, up-to-date, reliable, and complete information. No warranties of any kind are declared or implied. Readers acknowledge that the author is not engaged in the rendering of legal, financial, medical, or professional advice. The content within this book has been derived from various sources. Please consult a licensed professional before attempting any techniques outlined in this book.

By reading this document, the reader agrees that under no circumstances is the author responsible for any losses, direct or indirect, that are incurred as a result of the use of the information contained within this document, including, but not limited to, errors, omissions, or inaccuracies.

CONTENTS

1865 POSITIVE AFFIRMATIONS FOR BLACK WOMEN

Introduction	5
Frequently Asked Questions About Affirmations	9
1. Understanding Positive Affirmations	13
2. The Transformative Power of Affirmations for Black Women	17
3. Affirmations for Self-Love and Acceptance	21
4. Affirmations for Healing: Mind, Body, and Spirit	26
5. Affirmations for Physical Health and Wellness	32
Affirming Our Journey: A Moment of Reflection	35
6. Affirmations for Healthy, Fulfilling Relationships	37
7. Affirmations for Career Success and Fulfillment	45
8. Affirmations for Abundance and Prosperity	51
9. Affirmations for Self-Confidence and Empowerment	57
Conclusion: Embracing Your Affirmed Self - A Lifelong Journey	63
A Call to Action: Share Your Light	67
Affirmation Journal Section	69
Bibliography	71

1865 POSITIVE AFFIRMATIONS FOR BLACK WOMEN

Introduction	77
1. Affirmations 1 - 250	81
2. Affirmations 251 - 500	104
3. Affirmations 501 - 750	130
4. Affirmations 751 - 1001	154
Conclusion	179
Bibliography	183

1865 POSITIVE AFFIRMATIONS
— FOR —
BLACK WOMEN

Cultivate *Wealth*, *Wellness*, and *Winning Relationships* with an Empowered Mindset

IMANI ELKINS

For the phenomenal black women in my life who have inspired me with their strength, resilience, and love - and for every black woman who needs a reminder of her inherent magic and worth, this book is for you.

INTRODUCTION

"The only limit to the height of your achievements is the reach of your dreams and your willingness to work for them." - Michelle Obama.

In 1865, the 13th Amendment was ratified, marking the official end of slavery in the United States (National Archives, 2022). For black women, this date represents a turning point in a long and ongoing fight for liberation. It symbolizes the resilience, strength, and unbreakable spirit that have sustained us through centuries of oppression.

Yet more than 150 years later, black women still face systemic barriers and daily challenges that can make it difficult to cultivate self-love, manifest our deepest desires, and show up as our fullest selves. From the workplace to our relationships to our inner lives, we are bombarded with messages that we are not enough.

Affirmations are a powerful tool for rejecting these toxic messages and claiming our inherent worth. By intentionally choosing thoughts that uplift and empower us, we can literally rewire our brains to focus on our strengths, gifts, and highest potential. We can transform our lives from the inside out.

This book is both an introduction to the practice of affirmations and a practical guide for black women who want to use this tool to create meaningful change. You'll gain a deeper understanding of the science behind affirmations, learn how to craft affirmations that resonate with your personal experience, and discover hundreds of sample affirmations for different areas of life, from self-love and confidence to career, relationships, health, and more.

Whether you're new to affirmations or have been practicing for years, this book meets you where you are. It's designed to be a resource you can return to again and again for inspiration, encouragement, and practical tools to navigate life's challenges and triumphs.

Most importantly, this book is a celebration of black women's magic, brilliance, and unshakeable spirit. It's a reminder that we are the descendants of warriors, queens, and trailblazers who refused to be silenced. When we affirm our worth and claim our power, we honor their legacy and pave the way for future generations.

So take a deep breath, settle in, and get ready to embark on a transformative journey. You are exactly where you're meant to be. Let's begin.

"FROM SKEPTIC TO BELIEVER: HOW AFFIRMATIONS CHANGED MY LIFE"

I remember the first time I heard about affirmations. I was in my early twenties, struggling with self-doubt and negative self-talk that had plagued me since childhood. As a young black woman trying to navigate college and career aspirations, I often felt like an imposter, constantly questioning my worth and abilities.

One day, a friend recommended I try using affirmations to shift my mindset. I was skeptical at first, thinking it sounded too good to be true. How could simply repeating positive phrases change the deeply ingrained beliefs I held about myself?

But I decided to give it a try. I started small, writing down a few affirmations on Post-it notes and sticking them on my bathroom mirror. Every morning, I would look myself in the eye and repeat phrases like *"I am capable and worthy of success"* and *"I trust in my unique gifts and talents."*

At first, it felt awkward and forced. But as I continued the practice, I began to notice subtle shifts in my thinking. When self-doubt crept in, I found myself naturally replacing those negative thoughts with the affirmations I had been practicing. I started to feel more confident in my abilities and more resilient in the face of challenges.

Over time, the practice of affirmations became a daily ritual that transformed not just my mindset but my entire life. I began to attract opportunities and relationships that aligned with my new, empowered beliefs about myself. I took bold risks in my career and personal life, knowing that I had the strength and wisdom to handle whatever came my way.

Looking back, I'm amazed at how something as simple as repeating positive phrases could have such a profound impact on my life. Affirmations have become a powerful tool for me, helping me to navigate the ups and downs of life with greater ease and resilience.

Through this book, I hope to share the incredible gift of affirmations with other black women who may be struggling with similar doubts and fears. I truly believe that by changing our self-talk, we can change our lives – and together, we can create a world where every black woman knows her inherent worth and power.

FREQUENTLY ASKED QUESTIONS ABOUT AFFIRMATIONS

As you embark on your affirmation journey, you may have questions or concerns. Here are answers to some common questions, backed by research and expert insights:

Q1: Do affirmations really work?

A: Yes, research supports the effectiveness of affirmations. A study published in the journal Social Cognitive and Affective Neuroscience found that self-affirmation activates brain circuits associated with self-related processing and reward (Cascio et al., 2016). Another study in the Personality and Social Psychology Bulletin demonstrated that affirmations can protect against the negative effects of stress on problem-solving performance (Creswell et al., 2013).

Q2: How long does it take for affirmations to work?

A: The time frame can vary for each individual. Some people report feeling a shift in their mindset within a few days, while for others it may take weeks or months of consistent practice. A study in the Journal of Personality and Social Psychology found that a brief affirmation intervention had effects that persisted for months and even years (Cohen et al., 2009).

Q3: What if I don't believe my affirmations?

A: It's normal to feel some resistance at first, especially if the affirmations contradict long-held negative beliefs. The key is consistency and patience. Start with affirmations that feel believable and gradually work up to more ambitious ones. Research suggests that even if you don't fully believe the affirmations at first, the repeated exposure can still have positive effects over time (Wood et al., 2009).

Q4: How often should I practice affirmations?

A: Daily practice is ideal. A study in the journal PLOS ONE found that participants who practiced self-affirmation for a few minutes each day showed significant improvements in their ability to solve problems under stress (Creswell et al., 2013). Find a time that works for you, whether it's first thing in the morning, during your lunch break, or before bed.

Q5: Can affirmations help with specific issues like anxiety or low self-esteem?

A: Yes, research indicates that affirmations can be beneficial for a range of psychological issues. A study in the journal Psychological Science found that self-affirmation was effective in reducing symptoms of stress (Sherman et al., 2009). Another study in the Journal of Personality and Social Psychology showed that affirmations could boost self-esteem and reduce social anxiety (Stapel & van der Linde, 2011).

Q6: Are some affirmations more effective than others?

A: The most effective affirmations are those that are personally meaningful and relevant to your goals and values. Research in the Personality and Social Psychology Bulletin suggests that affirmations are most powerful when they reinforce a person's core values (Crocker et al., 2008).

Remember, affirmations are a tool for personal growth and empowerment. While they can be incredibly powerful, they work best when combined with action and a genuine commitment to change. Be patient with yourself, stay consistent in your practice, and don't hesitate to seek professional help if you're dealing with serious mental health concerns.

1

UNDERSTANDING POSITIVE AFFIRMATIONS

"Watch your thoughts, they become your words; watch your words, they become your actions; watch your actions, they become your habits; watch your habits, they become your character; watch your character, it becomes your destiny." - Lao Tzu.

This ancient wisdom captures the essence of why affirmations are so powerful. Our thoughts shape our reality in profound and often unconscious ways. When we change our thoughts, we set in motion a chain reaction that can transform every aspect of our lives.

At their core, affirmations are simply statements that we repeat to ourselves, either silently or out loud, to challenge limiting beliefs and cultivate a more empowered mindset (Kross et al., 2014). By consciously choosing words that affirm our worth, strengths, and desires, we train our brains to focus on possibilities rather than limitations.

The science behind affirmations is well-established. Studies using MRI scans have shown that affirmations activate the reward centers in our brains, releasing feel-good hormones like dopamine (Cascio et al., 2016). Over time, this positive reinforcement helps to override negative thought patterns and establish new neural pathways.

Affirmations have also been found to decrease stress, boost self-esteem, and improve academic performance (Sherman et al., 2013). When we affirm our values and identity, we become more resilient in the face of challenges and more likely to bounce back from setbacks.

But crafting effective affirmations requires more than just repeating generic positive phrases. The most powerful affirmations are:

- Stated in the present tense, as if they are already true.
- Focused on what you want rather than what you don't want.
- Infused with positive emotion and sensory details.
- Aligned with your core values and authentic self.
- Repeated regularly and with conviction.

For example, rather than saying, "I will be more confident," a well-crafted affirmation might be: "*I am standing tall and speaking my truth with clarity and conviction. I trust my inherent wisdom and value my unique perspective.*"

As you read through the affirmations in the coming chapters, take note of the ones that resonate most deeply with you. You might write them down, post them somewhere visible, or record yourself saying them out loud. Experiment with different wording and phrasing until you find affirmations that feel authentic and inspiring to you.

Remember, affirmations are not about bypassing or suppressing difficult emotions. It's normal for your mind to resist or reject affirmations at first, especially if they clash with long-held negative beliefs. The key is to keep practicing, even if you don't fully believe the words yet. With time and repetition, your brain will start to accept the new messages as true.

Like any new habit, consistency is key. Aim to repeat your affirmations at least twice a day, ideally in the morning and before bed. You can also use them as a tool in the moment to reframe stressful situations or combat negative self-talk.

As you strengthen your affirmation practice, you may start to notice subtle shifts in your mood, energy, and interactions with others. You may feel more grounded, confident, and able to handle life's ups and downs with grace.

This is the power of affirmations: to help us become more aware of our thoughts and intentionally choose ones that support our growth and well-being. When we change our self-talk, we open up new possibilities for healing, connection, and success on our own terms.

"BREAKING FREE FROM LIMITING BELIEFS: HOW AFFIRMATIONS HELPED ME ACHIEVE MY DREAMS"

Jasmine had always dreamed of starting her own business, but fear and self-doubt held her back. As a single mother of two, she struggled to make ends meet and couldn't imagine finding the time or resources to pursue her entrepreneurial goals.

One day, while scrolling through social media, Jasmine came across a post about the power of affirmations. Intrigued, she started researching the topic and decided to give it a try. She began by writing down her biggest limiting beliefs about herself and her abilities, such as "I'm not smart enough to run a business" and "I don't have what it takes to succeed."

Next, Jasmine crafted affirmations to counteract each negative belief. She replaced *"I'm not smart enough"* with *"I am intelligent and capable of learning anything I set my mind to."* Instead of *"I don't have what it takes,"* she affirmed, *"I have unique gifts and talents that make me a powerful entrepreneur."*

Jasmine began repeating her affirmations daily, both in the morning and before bed. She also started visualizing herself as a successful business owner, imagining the pride and joy she would feel in creating something of her own.

As Jasmine continued her affirmation practice, she began to notice a shift in her mindset. The limiting beliefs that had once seemed so real started to lose their power, replaced by a growing sense of confidence and determination.

Inspired by her newfound self-belief, Jasmine took action towards her dream. She enrolled in online business courses, reached out to mentors for guidance, and started developing her product ideas. Every step of the way, she used affirmations to keep herself motivated and focused on her goals.

Six months later, Jasmine launched her own natural skincare line, fulfilling a lifelong dream. As she looked back on her journey, she realized that the power to achieve her goals had been within her all along – she simply needed to believe in herself enough to take the first step.

Jasmine's story is a powerful reminder that our thoughts and beliefs shape our reality. By using affirmations to break free from limiting beliefs, we open ourselves up to a world of possibilities and unlock our true potential.

2

THE TRANSFORMATIVE POWER OF AFFIRMATIONS FOR BLACK WOMEN

"I am deliberate and afraid of nothing." - Audre Lorde.

For black women, the practice of repeating empowering words to affirm our humanity is not a new phenomenon. African oral traditions have long used call and response, storytelling, and proverbs to instill values, preserve history, and celebrate community (Anyangwe, 2015).

During slavery, African Americans used spirituals and coded language to secretly communicate messages of resilience, faith, and liberation (Johnson, 2011). In the Jim Crow era, black women writers like Phyllis Wheatley and Zora Neale Hurston used their pens to assert their intellect and creativity in the face of racist stereotypes (McKissack & McKissack, 1995).

The 1970s saw the emergence of a new literary genre called affirmations, pioneered by black female writers like Toni Cade Bambara and June Jordan (Pippen, 2015). These writers used first-person mantras to speak life into their dreams and combat internalized oppression.

Today, black women continue to use affirmations as a tool for resistance and empowerment. From bestselling books like *"I'm Judging You"* by Luvvie Ajayi Jones to social media movements like *#BlackGirlMagic*, we are harnessing the power of our words to celebrate our strengths and dismantle limiting beliefs.

Research suggests that affirmations may be especially beneficial for black women who face unique stressors and challenges. A study by Settles et al. (2010) found that black women who used self-affirmations reported higher self-esteem and greater life satisfaction than those who did not. Another study by Jones et al. (2019) found that affirmations helped black college women combat impostor syndrome and feel more empowered in academic settings.

But the power of affirmations extends beyond the individual. When we, as black women, affirm our worth and uplift each other, we create a ripple effect that strengthens our families, communities, and movements for justice. We become role models for younger generations, showing them that they can dream big and achieve the impossible.

Take the story of Shirley Chisholm, the first black woman elected to Congress and the first to run for president. When asked how she had the audacity to seek the nation's highest office, Chisholm replied: *"I stand before you today as a candidate for the Democratic nomination for the Presidency of the United States. I am not the candidate of black America, although I am black and proud. I am not the candidate of the women's movement of this country, although I am a woman and I am equally proud of that. I am the candidate of the people of America."* (Chisholm, 1972, para. 1-2).

Chisholm's words were a powerful affirmation of her right to take up space and pursue her dreams, regardless of the limitations society tried to place on her. She paved the way for future generations of black women leaders, from Barbara Jordan to Kamala Harris.

As black women, we stand on the shoulders of giants like Shirley Chisholm. When we affirm our power, we honor their legacy and contribute to a long tradition of black women's resistance and resilience. We become the ancestors we want to see in the world.

So, how can you start incorporating affirmations into your daily life? Here are a few tips:

- 1.Identify your core values and beliefs. What matters most to you? What kind of person do you want to be? Use these as a guide for crafting affirmations that resonate with your authentic self.
- 2.Start small. Choose one or two affirmations to focus on each day or week. Repeat them to yourself when you wake up, before meals, or whenever you need a boost.
- 3.Use present tense and positive language. Frame your affirmations as if they are already true, and focus on what you want rather than what you don't want. For example: "I am grateful for my strong, healthy body" vs. "I am no longer stressed."
- 4.Engage your senses. Visualize yourself embodying the qualities you're affirming. What does it look like, feel like, sound like to be that version of yourself? The more vivid and specific, the better.
- 5.Find an accountability partner. Share your affirmations with a friend, family member, or therapist who can support you and help you stay motivated. You might even inspire them to start their own affirmation practice!
- 6.Be patient and consistent. Like any new habit, building an affirmation practice takes time and effort. Don't get discouraged if you miss a day or if the words feel awkward at first. Keep showing up for yourself with compassion and commitment.

Remember, affirmations are not a magic cure-all. They are one tool in a larger toolkit of self-care and personal growth. But when used regularly and with intention, they can be a powerful catalyst for transformation - not just for individuals but for entire communities.

As black women, we have a unique opportunity and responsibility to use our words for healing, empowerment, and collective liberation. When we affirm our magic, we create space for others to do the same. We become the change we wish to see in the world.

"SOJOURNER TRUTH: A LEGACY OF RESILIENCE AND POSITIVE SELF-TALK"

Sojourner Truth, born Isabella Baumfree, was an African American abolitionist and women's rights activist who lived in the 19th century. Born into slavery, Truth faced unimaginable hardships and challenges throughout her life, including being separated from her family, enduring physical abuse, and fighting for her freedom in court.

Despite the many obstacles she faced, Truth remained resilient and unwavering in her conviction that she was a child of God, deserving of love and respect. Her speeches and writings are filled with powerful affirmations of her worth and purpose, such as *"I am a woman's rights"* and *"I sell the shadow to support the substance."*

One of Truth's most famous speeches, *"Ain't I a Woman?"* delivered at the Ohio Women's Rights Convention in 1851, is a testament to the power of positive self-talk in the face of oppression. In the speech, Truth affirms her own humanity and the humanity of all women, regardless of race or class.

"That man over there says that women need to be helped into carriages, and lifted over ditches, and to have the best place everywhere," Truth declared. *"Nobody ever helps me into carriages, or over mud-puddles, or gives me any best place! And ain't I a woman?"*

Through her words and actions, Truth challenged the negative stereotypes and limiting beliefs that society placed on black women. She refused to be silenced or diminished, instead using her voice to affirm her own worth and fight for the rights of others.

Truth's legacy of resilience and positive self-talk continues to inspire generations of black women today. Her example reminds us that no matter the challenges we face, we have the power within ourselves to rise above and create change. By affirming our own humanity and the humanity of others, we carry on the work that Truth and so many other brave women began.

3

AFFIRMATIONS FOR SELF-LOVE AND ACCEPTANCE

"Loving ourselves works miracles in our lives." - *Louise Hay.*

Self-love is a radical act for black women. In a society that constantly tells us we are too much and not enough, choosing to embrace ourselves exactly as we are is a form of resistance. It's a way of saying, "I am worthy of love and respect, even if the world doesn't always reflect that back to me."

But self-love is not always easy, especially if we've experienced trauma, discrimination, or marginalization. Many of us have internalized negative messages about our worth, appearance, abilities, or lovability. We may struggle with impostor syndrome, perfectionism, or people-pleasing tendencies that make it difficult to prioritize our own needs and desires.

That's where affirmations come in. By repeating positive statements about ourselves, we begin to chip away at the negative beliefs that hold us back. We train our brains to focus on our strengths, talents, and inherent worth. We cultivate a sense of self-compassion and acceptance that allows us to show up more fully in our lives and relationships.

Research has shown that self-affirmation can buffer against the negative effects of stereotype threat and discrimination (Sherman & Cohen, 2006). When we affirm our values and identity, we become more resilient in the face of external challenges and less likely to internalize negative feedback.

Self-love affirmations can be particularly powerful for black women, who face unique pressures and expectations around beauty, sexuality, and femininity. By affirming our right to take up space, define our own standards of attractiveness, and express ourselves authentically, we reclaim our bodies and minds from oppressive systems.

HERE ARE SOME EXAMPLES OF SELF-LOVE AFFIRMATIONS FOR BLACK WOMEN:

- I am deeply loved and worthy of love, just as I am.
- My beauty shines from the inside out.
- I honor my body's wisdom and trust its messages.
- I am allowed to rest and receive without guilt.
- My feelings are valid and deserve to be expressed.
- I forgive myself for past mistakes and trust in my ability to learn and grow.
- I am grateful for my unique talents and gifts.
- I am more than enough in every way.
- I release the need for perfection and embrace my humanity.
- I choose to be kind and compassionate towards myself.

As you repeat these affirmations, take a moment to really feel them in your body. Place a hand on your heart, take a deep breath, and imagine the words sinking into every cell. Notice any resistance or discomfort that arises and meet it with curiosity and compassion.

Remember, self-love is not a destination but an ongoing practice. Some days, it may feel effortless, while other days, it may be a struggle just to look in the mirror. The key is to keep showing up for yourself, even and especially when it's hard.

One powerful way to cultivate self-love is through self-care rituals that honor your mind, body, and spirit. This might look like:

- Taking a relaxing bath with candles and essential oils.
- Dancing or singing along to your favorite music.
- Nourishing your body with healthy, delicious foods.
- Spending time in nature and soaking up the beauty around you.
- Journaling about your hopes, dreams, fears, and triumphs.
- Saying "no" to activities or relationships that drain you.
- Surrounding yourself with positive, uplifting people who see and celebrate your greatness.

As you incorporate more acts of self-love into your daily life, you may begin to notice subtle shifts in how you show up in the world. You may find yourself speaking up more at work, setting healthier boundaries in relationships, or pursuing your passions with greater confidence and clarity. You may inspire others to start their own self-love journey, creating a ripple effect of healing in your community.

Remember, self-love is not selfish or indulgent. It's a necessary foundation for living a fulfilling, purposeful life and making a positive impact in the world. When we fill our own cups first, we have more to give to others.

As the brilliant Audre Lorde once said, *"Caring for myself is not self-indulgence, it is self-preservation, and that is an act of political warfare."* (Lorde, 1988, p. 131)

By affirming our inherent worth and prioritizing our well-being, we are not only caring for ourselves - we are fighting for a world where all black women can thrive. We are claiming our rightful place in a long legacy of resistance, resilience, and radical self-love.

So start today. Look in the mirror and affirm your beauty, power, and limitless potential. Treat yourself with the tenderness and compassion you deserve. Surround yourself with reminders of your greatness.

You are a masterpiece in progress. You are a divine work of art. You are loved, lovable, and worthy of every good thing. Believe it, embody it, and watch your life transform in beautiful ways.

"FALLING IN LOVE WITH MYSELF: HOW AFFIRMATIONS HELPED ME EMBRACE MY WORTH"

Growing up, I struggled with low self-esteem and a constant feeling of unworthiness. As a dark-skinned black girl in a society that glorified light skin and European features, I internalized the message that I was somehow less beautiful and less valuable than my peers.

These feelings followed me into adulthood, impacting my relationships and career. I found myself settling for less than I deserved, both personally and professionally, because I didn't believe I was worthy of more.

The turning point came when I started therapy and discovered the power of affirmations. My therapist encouraged me to start each day by looking in the mirror and saying something positive about myself, no matter how small. At first, it felt awkward and insincere, but I committed to the practice.

I started with simple affirmations like *"I am enough"* and *"I am worthy of love and respect."* Over time, I began to craft more specific affirmations tailored to my unique qualities and goals, such as *"I am a talented writer with a powerful voice"* and *"I attract healthy, loving relationships into my life."*

As I continued affirming my worth, I began to notice a shift in how I saw myself. The negative self-talk that had once dominated my thoughts began to fade, replaced by a growing sense of self-love and acceptance. I started setting boundaries in my relationships and pursuing my passions with greater confidence.

One of the most transformative moments came when I decided to do a boudoir photoshoot as a gift to myself. As I posed in lingerie and saw the beautiful, powerful images that resulted, I realized that the love and acceptance I had been seeking was within me all along.

Affirmations helped me to embrace my unique beauty, inside and out. They taught me that my worth is not determined by societal standards or external validation, but by the love and respect, I show myself. Today, I continue to use affirmations as a tool for self-care and empowerment, reminding myself daily of my inherent value.

To any black woman struggling with self-doubt or feelings of unworthiness, I encourage you to try the practice of affirmations. Start small with simple phrases that resonate with you, and build from there. Remember that you are the expert on your own experience and what you need to feel loved and supported.

As you continue on your journey of self-love, know that you are not alone. You are part of a long lineage of black women who have fought to affirm their humanity and worth in a world that often seeks to deny it. By embracing your own beauty and power, you honor their legacy and pave the way for future generations to do the same.

4

AFFIRMATIONS FOR HEALING: MIND, BODY, AND SPIRIT

"Healing takes time, and asking for help is a courageous step."
— Mariska Hargitay.

As black women, we carry the weight of generations of trauma in our bodies, minds, and spirits. From the horrific legacy of slavery and Jim Crow to the ongoing violence of racism, sexism, and oppression, we have endured unimaginable pain and loss. This intergenerational trauma can manifest in physical and mental health disparities, as well as a deep sense of unworthiness or disconnection from our authentic selves.

But we are also the descendants of healers, warriors, and survivors. We have inherited a profound capacity for resilience, creativity, and transformation. When we turn our attention inward and commit to our own healing, we tap into this ancestral wisdom and strength. We become vessels for collective liberation and change.

One powerful tool for healing is the practice of affirmations. By repeating positive, uplifting statements about our bodies, minds, and spirits, we begin to rewire our neural pathways and release limiting beliefs. We cultivate a sense of safety, trust, and wholeness that allows us to navigate life's challenges with greater ease and grace.

Research has shown that affirmations can have a measurable impact on physical health outcomes. In one study, breast cancer survivors who practiced self-affirmation experienced less fatigue and depression, as well as greater self-compassion and spiritual well-being (Sherman et al., 2017). Another study found that self-affirmation reduced the impact of racial discrimination on hypertension risk among African American participants (Johnson et al., 2019).

But the benefits of affirmations extend beyond the physical realm. By affirming our mental and emotional well-being, we create space for processing difficult emotions, setting healthy boundaries, and communicating our needs with clarity and compassion. We learn to treat ourselves with the same kindness and understanding we extend to others.

HERE ARE SOME EXAMPLES OF AFFIRMATIONS FOR HEALING THE MIND, BODY, AND SPIRIT:

- I trust in my body's innate wisdom and capacity to heal.
- I release all shame, guilt, and self-judgment around my health and well-being.
- I nourish myself with thoughts, foods, and experiences that uplift and energize me.
- I breathe deeply and fully, letting go of tension with each exhale.
- I am open to receiving support and guidance from others on my healing journey.
- I forgive myself for any ways I have neglected or mistreated my body in the past.
- I am grateful for the resilience and strength of my ancestors, which flows through me now.
- I release any pain or trauma that is not mine to carry.

- I trust in the perfect timing and unfolding of my healing process.
- I am a powerful creator of my own reality, and I choose thoughts that support my highest good.

As you work with these affirmations, remember that healing is not a linear process. There may be days when you feel strong and empowered and others when old wounds resurface, or new challenges arise. This is normal and natural. The key is to meet yourself with compassion and patience, remembering that every step forward is worth celebrating.

One way to deepen your affirmation practice is to pair it with other healing modalities, such as:

- Mindfulness meditation, which helps cultivate present-moment awareness and emotional regulation (Tenfelde et al., 2014).
- Yoga, which can alleviate symptoms of depression, anxiety, and PTSD (Macy et al., 2018).
- Expressive arts, such as painting, dancing, or writing, which provide a creative outlet for painful emotions and experiences (Stuckey & Nobel, 2010).
- Therapy or counseling, especially with a culturally competent provider who understands the unique challenges facing black women (Woods-Giscombé & Black, 2010).
- Connecting with nature, whether through gardening, hiking, or simply spending time outdoors, which can boost mood and promote relaxation (McCallum & McLaren, 2011).

Remember, healing is not about fixing yourself or achieving some state of perfection. It's about coming home to yourself, again and again, with honesty, curiosity, and love. It's about reclaiming your birthright to joy, pleasure, and wholeness, even in a world that often denies your humanity.

As the poet Nayyirah Waheed writes, "Just because someone has broken your heart, does not mean you are broken. Being broken is when you give up on love." (Waheed, 2013)

By affirming your worthiness and committing to your own healing, you are choosing love - for yourself, your community, and the world. You are planting seeds of resilience and resistance that will blossom for generations to come.

So take a deep breath, place a hand on your heart, and repeat after me: I am worthy of healing. I am capable of transformation. I am enough, just as I am. And so it is.

"HEALING FROM THE INSIDE OUT: HOW AFFIRMATIONS SUPPORTED MY HEALTH JOURNEY"

When Tanya was diagnosed with an autoimmune disorder in her early thirties, she felt like her world had been turned upside down. As a busy professional and mother of two, she had always prided herself on her ability to handle anything life threw her way. But now, faced with chronic pain and fatigue, she found herself struggling to keep up with the demands of daily life.

Tanya's doctor recommended a combination of medication and lifestyle changes to manage her symptoms, but she knew she needed more than just physical treatment to truly heal. That's when she discovered the power of affirmations.

At first, Tanya was skeptical. She had always been a practical, no-nonsense kind of person, and the idea of repeating positive phrases to herself felt a bit woo-woo. But as she began researching the science behind affirmations and their impact on the mind-body connection, she decided to give it a try.

Tanya started by creating a list of affirmations specifically related to her health, such as *"My body is a powerful healer"* and *"I trust in my body's ability to find balance and vitality."* She set a reminder on her phone to repeat these affirmations every morning and evening, as well as whenever she felt pain or frustration with her condition.

As Tanya continued her affirmation practice, she began to notice subtle shifts in her mindset and energy levels. Instead of getting caught up in negative self-talk about her limitations, she found herself focusing on her body's innate wisdom and resilience. She started to approach her treatment plan with a greater sense of empowerment and self-compassion.

Tanya also used affirmations to cultivate a deeper sense of connection and gratitude for her body. She began thanking her body for all the ways it supported her, even on difficult days. She affirmed her commitment to nourishing herself with healthy foods, gentle movement, and plenty of rest.

Over time, Tanya found that her affirmation practice not only supported her physical healing but also helped her to develop a more loving, accepting relationship with her body. She learned to honor her own needs and boundaries, both in her health journey and in her relationships with others.

Today, Tanya continues to use affirmations as part of her daily self-care routine. She knows that healing is not a linear process and that there will always be ups and downs along the way. But by affirming her body's innate wisdom and her own worthiness of care and support, she has found a powerful tool for navigating whatever challenges come her way.

Tanya's story is a reminder that true healing often begins from within. By using affirmations to shift our mindset and cultivate a more loving relationship with our bodies, we tap into a deep well of resilience and self-compassion. We learn to trust in our own inner guidance and advocate for our needs with greater clarity and confidence.

If you are struggling with a health challenge, whether physical or mental, I encourage you to try incorporating affirmations into your healing journey. Remember that your body is always working for you, even when it doesn't feel that way. By affirming your body's inherent wisdom and your own worthiness of care, you create a foundation of love and support that can carry you through even the toughest times.

5

AFFIRMATIONS FOR PHYSICAL HEALTH AND WELLNESS

"To keep the body in good health is a duty... otherwise we shall not be able to keep our mind strong and clear." – Buddha

As black women, our relationship with our bodies is complex and often fraught with societal pressures, historical trauma, and systemic health disparities. Yet our bodies are powerful, resilient temples that deserve love, care, and celebration. Affirmations can be a transformative tool in reclaiming our physical health and cultivating a positive relationship with our bodies.

Research has shown that positive self-talk and affirmations can have tangible effects on physical health outcomes. A study by Creswell et al. (2014) found that self-affirmation was associated with reduced stress reactivity and lower cortisol responses in participants. Another study by Sherman et al. (2009) demonstrated that self-affirmation interventions could increase physical activity levels in sedentary individuals.

By affirming our body's strength, wisdom, and capacity for healing, we can shift our mindset from one of struggle or deprivation to one of empowerment and self-love. This shift can lead to more consistent healthy behaviors, reduced stress, and improved overall well-being.

Here are some powerful affirmations for physical health and wellness:

- I love and appreciate my body for all it does for me.
- My body is strong, resilient, and capable of healing itself.
- I nourish my body with healthy foods that energize and strengthen me.
- I enjoy moving my body and staying active.
- I listen to my body's signals and honor its needs for rest and recovery.
- I am worthy of excellent health care and advocate for my needs.
- My body is a masterpiece, regardless of its shape or size.
- I release any negative beliefs about my body and embrace self-love.
- I am in control of my health and make choices that support my well-being.
- I radiate health, vitality, and confidence from the inside out.

As you work with these affirmations, remember that true health encompasses more than just physical fitness or a number on a scale. It's about cultivating a loving, respectful relationship with your body and honoring its unique needs and rhythms.

Here are some additional practices to enhance your physical wellness affirmation practice:

1. Body Gratitude Ritual: Each morning or evening, stand in front of a mirror and name three things you appreciate about your body. This could be its strength, its resilience, or even something as simple as the color of your eyes or the curve of your smile.
2. Mindful Movement: As you exercise or stretch, repeat affirmations that celebrate your body's strength and

capabilities. This can help shift your focus from changing your body to appreciating what it can do.
3. Nourishment Affirmations: Before meals, take a moment to affirm your intention to nourish your body with love and care. This can help foster a healthier relationship with food and eating.
4. Health Visualization: Spend a few minutes each day visualizing yourself in perfect health, filled with energy and vitality. Pair this visualization with affirmations to reinforce the image of wellness in your mind.
5. Self-Care Affirmations: As you engage in self-care activities like taking a bath, applying lotion, or getting a massage, repeat affirmations that reinforce your worthiness of care and nurturing.

Remember, your journey to physical wellness is unique and personal. Be patient and compassionate with yourself as you work to shift your mindset and habits. Celebrate every small step towards greater health and self-love, knowing that you are worthy of vibrant well-being in all its forms.

AFFIRMING OUR JOURNEY: A MOMENT OF REFLECTION

"You've been assigned this mountain to show others it can be moved." - Mel Robbins.

As we reach the midpoint of our journey together through the transformative power of affirmations, I invite you to take a moment to reflect on how far you've come. By engaging with the practices and insights in these pages, you are taking a courageous step towards claiming your inherent worth, power, and potential as a black woman.

I know that this work is not always easy. It requires us to confront limiting beliefs, heal past wounds, and step outside our comfort zones. But I also know that the rewards are immeasurable. When we commit to affirming our greatness and showing up fully in our lives, we become unstoppable forces for positive change - in our own lives and in the world around us.

As you continue on this path of self-discovery and empowerment, I encourage you to take a moment to celebrate your progress and insights so far. What affirmations have resonated most deeply with you? What new perspectives or habits have you begun to incorporate into your daily life? What moments of joy, connection, or growth have you experienced as a result?

I also invite you to share your journey with others. By leaving an honest review of this book and the impact it has had on your life, you can inspire and encourage other black women who may be struggling with similar challenges. Your voice and your story matter, and they have the power to create ripples of hope and healing in our communities.

To leave a review, simply scan the QR code

Remember, you are not alone on this journey. You are part of a long lineage of black women who have affirmed their worth and changed the world through the power of their words and actions. By claiming your own unique magic and purpose, you honor their legacy and pave the way for future generations to do the same.

So keep shining, keep affirming, and keep rising. The best is yet to come.

With gratitude and solidarity,

Imani

6

AFFIRMATIONS FOR HEALTHY, FULFILLING RELATIONSHIPS

"You yourself, as much as anybody in the entire universe, deserve your love and affection." - Buddha

As social beings, our relationships play a vital role in our overall well-being and happiness. From the intimate bonds we share with partners and family to the connections we forge in our communities and workplaces, our relationships shape our sense of belonging, purpose, and identity.

But for many black women, cultivating healthy, fulfilling relationships can be a challenge. We may struggle with setting boundaries, communicating our needs, or trusting others due to past experiences of trauma, betrayal, or abandonment. We may feel pressure to be strong, independent, and self-sacrificing, even at the expense of our own well-being. And we may internalize messages from society that we are unworthy of love, respect, or partnership.

Affirmations can be a powerful tool for shifting these limiting beliefs and attracting more positive, supportive relationships into our lives. By focusing our thoughts and energy on what we desire in our connections with others, we begin to vibrate at a higher frequency and draw in people and experiences that align with our values.

Research has shown that affirmations can increase feelings of self-worth and reduce the impact of social threats on interpersonal relationships (Cohen & Sherman, 2014). When we affirm our inherent lovability and value, we become less reactive to rejection or criticism and more able to show up authentically in our interactions with others.

Affirmations can also help us communicate more effectively and compassionately in our relationships. By focusing on positive, solution-oriented language, we create a safe space for honest dialogue and mutual understanding. We learn to express our needs and desires clearly, without blame or judgment, and to listen deeply to the needs and desires of others.

HERE ARE SOME EXAMPLES OF AFFIRMATIONS FOR CULTIVATING HEALTHY, FULFILLING RELATIONSHIPS:

- I am worthy of love, respect, and compassion in all my relationships.
- I attract partners who appreciate and support my authentic self.
- I communicate my boundaries and needs with clarity and confidence.
- I release any past hurts or resentments that block me from giving and receiving love.
- I trust in the divine timing and purpose of all my relationships.
- I am a compassionate, understanding, and supportive friend/partner/family member.
- I surround myself with people who inspire me to be my best self.
- I am grateful for the lessons and blessings in all my relationships, past and present.

- I forgive myself and others for any mistakes or misunderstandings, and I choose to move forward with love.
- I am open to receiving love and support from unexpected sources.

As you repeat these affirmations, take a moment to visualize yourself embodying the qualities you desire in your relationships. See yourself engaging in honest, heartfelt conversations with loved ones. Picture yourself setting healthy boundaries with ease and grace. Feel the warmth and comfort of being surrounded by people who truly see and appreciate you.

Remember, cultivating healthy relationships is an ongoing practice, not a destination. It requires patience, self-awareness, and a willingness to learn and grow. There may be moments of discomfort or vulnerability as you break old patterns and try new ways of relating. But by staying committed to your own growth and healing, you create space for more authentic, fulfilling connections to blossom.

In addition to affirmations, there are many other tools and practices that can support healthy relationships, such as:

- Nonviolent communication (NVC), a framework for expressing needs and feelings without blame or criticism (Rosenberg, 2015)
- Couples therapy or relationship coaching, especially with a provider who understands the unique dynamics facing black women (Kelly et al., 2018)
- Joining a support group or sisterhood circle, where you can share your experiences and receive guidance and encouragement from other black women (Neal-Barnett et al., 2011)
- Practicing self-care and setting aside regular time for your own hobbies, passions, and personal growth (Bryant-Davis, 2013)

Remember, you are not alone on this journey. As black women, we come from a long lineage of resilient, loving, and powerful ancestors who fought for the right to live and love freely. By honoring our own needs and desires in relationships, we continue this legacy and pave the way for future generations to thrive.

So take a deep breath, call in the love and support of your ancestors, and repeat after me: I am worthy of healthy, fulfilling relationships. I am surrounded by love, respect, and compassion. I am open to giving and receiving love in all its forms. And so it is.

"ATTRACTING LOVE AND HEALING: HOW AFFIRMATIONS TRANSFORMED MY RELATIONSHIPS"

When Simone first began using affirmations to improve her relationships, she was at a low point in her love life. After a string of toxic relationships and painful breakups, she found herself feeling hopeless and unworthy of the kind of love she truly desired.

As a child of divorce and a survivor of domestic violence, Simone had internalized a lot of negative beliefs about relationships and her own lovability. She often felt like she was *"too much"* or *"not enough"* for partners and struggled with feelings of jealousy and insecurity.

When a friend recommended using affirmations to shift her mindset and attract healthier relationships, Simone was initially resistant. She had tried positive thinking before, but it always felt like a superficial band-aid rather than a true solution.

But as Simone began researching the power of affirmations and how they could rewire the brain for greater self-love and compassion, she decided to give it a try. She started by writing down her deepest fears and negative beliefs about relationships, such as *"I am unlovable"* and *"All men will eventually leave me."*

Next, Simone crafted affirmations to counter each negative belief, such as *"I am worthy of deep, unconditional love"* and *"I trust in the divine timing of my romantic journey."* She began repeating these affirmations daily, both in the morning and before bed, as well as whenever feelings of insecurity or self-doubt arose.

As Simone continued her affirmation practice, she began to notice a shift in how she approached relationships. Instead of seeking validation or trying to change herself to fit someone else's desires, she started prioritizing her own needs and boundaries. She became more discerning about the kind of partners she allowed into her life, focusing on those who treated her with respect and kindness.

Simone also used affirmations to heal old wounds and traumas related to past relationships. She affirmed her own resilience and strength, reminding herself that she had survived difficult experiences and come out stronger. She practiced forgiveness and compassion towards herself and others, releasing the burden of resentment and anger.

Over time, Simone found that her relationships began to reflect the love and respect she was cultivating within herself. She attracted a partner who supported her dreams and cherished her for exactly who she was. She deepened her friendships and family connections, learning to communicate her needs and boundaries with greater clarity and confidence.

Today, Simone continues to use affirmations as a tool for maintaining healthy, fulfilling relationships. She knows that true love starts with self-love and that by affirming her own worth and lovability, she creates a foundation for authentic, supportive connections with others.

Simone's story is a powerful reminder that the quality of our relationships often reflects the relationship we have with ourselves. By using affirmations to heal past wounds, set healthy boundaries, and cultivate self-love, we attract people and experiences that align with our deepest values and desires.

If you find yourself struggling in your relationships, whether romantic or platonic, I encourage you to try incorporating affirmations into your daily practice. Start by identifying the negative beliefs or patterns that may be holding you back, and craft affirmations that affirm your worth, lovability, and right to healthy connections.

Remember that healing and growth take time and that there will be ups and downs along the way. But by committing to your own self-love and empowerment, you create a ripple effect of positivity that touches every area of your life, including your relationships. Trust in your own journey, and know that you are deserving of all the love and support you desire.

"FINDING MY VOICE: HOW AFFIRMATIONS EMPOWERED ME TO LAUNCH MY DREAM BUSINESS"

When Zara first stumbled upon the concept of affirmations, she was at a crossroads in her career. After years of working in corporate marketing, she felt unfulfilled and disconnected from her true passions. Deep down, Zara had always dreamed of starting her own business - a natural hair care line that celebrated the beauty and diversity of black women's hair. But fear, self-doubt, and limiting beliefs held her back from taking the leap.

"I kept telling myself that I wasn't ready, that I didn't have enough experience or resources to start a business," Zara recalls. *"I was afraid of failing and letting down my family, who had sacrificed so much for my education and career."*

It was during this period of uncertainty that Zara discovered the power of affirmations. Intrigued by the idea that she could rewire her thoughts and beliefs, she decided to give it a try. She started with simple affirmations like *"I am capable of creating a successful business"* and *"I have valuable skills and ideas to share with the world."*

At first, the affirmations felt awkward and forced. But Zara committed to repeating them daily, both in the morning and before bed. She also started a journal where she would write down her affirmations and reflect on any resistance or doubts that came up.

As weeks turned into months, Zara began to notice subtle shifts in her mindset and behavior. She found herself taking small but significant steps towards her dream - researching the natural hair care market, attending entrepreneurship workshops, and even experimenting with product formulations in her kitchen.

"The affirmations helped me tap into a confidence and courage I didn't know I had," Zara explains. *"Instead of focusing on all the reasons why I couldn't start a business, I started to see possibilities and opportunities everywhere."*

One of the most powerful moments in Zara's journey came when she crafted an affirmation specifically related to her business vision: *"I am the founder of a thriving natural hair care brand that empowers black women to embrace their natural beauty."* As she repeated this affirmation daily, Zara found herself becoming more and more aligned with this vision of herself as a successful entrepreneur.

With her newfound confidence and clarity, Zara took the bold step of quitting her corporate job to focus full-time on launching her business. It wasn't always easy - there were moments of doubt, setbacks, and financial strain. But Zara used her affirmations as a anchor, reminding herself of her worth, capability, and vision even in the face of challenges.

Two years later, Zara's natural hair care line has become a beloved brand in the black community, known for its high-quality, innovative products and empowering message. Her business has been featured in major publications and has a growing, loyal customer base.

"Looking back, I realize that the biggest obstacle to my success was my own limiting beliefs," Zara reflects. *"Affirmations helped me rewrite the story I was telling myself and step into my power as a black female entrepreneur. Now, I make sure to share the power of affirmations with every aspiring business owner I meet, especially other black women who might be doubting their abilities or worth."*

Zara's story is a powerful reminder that our thoughts and beliefs shape our reality. By using affirmations to overcome self-doubt and cultivate a success mindset, we can unlock our full potential and create the careers and businesses of our dreams. Remember, you have everything you need within you to succeed - sometimes, you just need to affirm it to believe it.

7

AFFIRMATIONS FOR CAREER SUCCESS AND FULFILLMENT

"Your work is to discover your work and then with all your heart give yourself to it." — Buddha.

For many black women, our careers are more than just a way to earn a living - they are a means of expressing our passions, making a difference in the world, and achieving financial security and independence. But as we strive to succeed in a business world that often undervalues and overlooks our contributions, we may face unique challenges and barriers.

From the intersecting pressures of racism and sexism to the lack of representation in leadership positions, black women often have to work twice as hard to be recognized and rewarded for our skills and talents. We may struggle with impostor syndrome, self-doubt, or burnout as we navigate workplace dynamics that were not designed with us in mind.

Affirmations can be a powerful tool for cultivating the mindset and confidence needed to thrive in our careers, no matter the obstacles we face. By focusing our thoughts and energy on our strengths, goals, and inherent worth, we train our brains to seek out opportunities for growth and success. We become more resilient in the face of setbacks and more able to advocate for ourselves and our ideas.

Research has shown that self-affirmation can improve problem-solving and creativity under stress (Creswell et al., 2013), as well as reduce the negative impact of stereotype threat on academic and professional performance (Martens et al., 2006). When we affirm our values and abilities, we are less likely to be derailed by external pressures or limiting beliefs.

Affirmations can also help us develop a growth mindset, which is the belief that our skills and intelligence can be developed through effort and learning (Dweck, 2016). With a growth mindset, we see challenges as opportunities to learn and improve rather than as threats to our self-worth. We become more open to feedback and more willing to take risks and try new things.

HERE ARE SOME EXAMPLES OF AFFIRMATIONS FOR CAREER SUCCESS AND FULFILLMENT:

- I am highly skilled, talented, and capable in my field.
- I trust my intuition and make decisions that align with my values and goals.
- I am confident in my ability to handle challenges and find creative solutions.
- I advocate for myself and my ideas with clarity and conviction.
- I attract opportunities and people that support my professional growth and success.
- I am grateful for my unique gifts and the value I bring to my work.
- I set healthy boundaries and prioritize self-care to avoid burnout.
- I celebrate my wins and learn from my losses with grace and resilience.

- I am open to feedback and use it to continuously improve and refine my skills.
- I am worthy of abundance, fulfillment, and joy in my career.

As you repeat these affirmations, take a moment to visualize yourself thriving in your dream career. See yourself confidently leading meetings, sharing your ideas, and collaborating with colleagues who value and respect your contributions. Feel the satisfaction and pride of doing work that truly lights you up and makes a difference in the world.

Remember, career success is not just about achieving external metrics like promotions or salary increases - it's about aligning your work with your values, passions, and purpose. It's about showing up authentically and bringing your whole self to the table, even when it feels vulnerable or risky.

In addition to affirmations, there are many other tools and strategies that can support your career growth and fulfillment, such as:

- Seeking out mentors, sponsors, and role models who can provide guidance, feedback, and opportunities for advancement (Davis, 2016)
- Building a strong professional network and leveraging social capital to access resources and support (Combs, 2003)
- Developing a personal brand and marketing yourself effectively through social media, speaking engagements, or thought leadership (Arruda, 2019)
- Continuously learning and upskilling through courses, workshops, or certifications (Sherman, 2018)
- Advocating for diversity, equity, and inclusion initiatives in your workplace or industry (Roberson, 2006)

Remember, your career journey is a marathon, not a sprint. There may be twists, turns, and detours along the way, but every experience is an opportunity for growth and self-discovery. Trust in your own unique path and timeline, and don't compare yourself to others.

As the incomparable Maya Angelou once said, *"You may encounter many defeats, but you must not be defeated. In fact, it may be necessary to encounter the defeats so you can know who you are, what you can rise from, how you can still come out of it."* (Angelou, 2014, p. 8)

By affirming your worth, talent, and potential, you become unstoppable in the face of any challenge or setback. You become a trailblazer and a changemaker, paving the way for future generations of black women to dream big and achieve the impossible.

So take a deep breath, connect with your purpose, and repeat after me: I am a powerful force for positive change in my career and in the world. I trust in my abilities and my journey. I am open to abundance, growth, and fulfillment in all areas of my life. And so it is.

"OWNING MY GREATNESS: HOW AFFIRMATIONS HELPED ME THRIVE IN MY CAREER"

When Jada first started her career in tech, she often felt like an outsider. As one of the few black women in her department, she struggled with imposter syndrome and self-doubt, questioning whether she truly belonged in such a competitive, fast-paced industry.

Jada had always been a high achiever, graduating at the top of her class and landing a prestigious internship at a major tech company. But as she navigated the challenges of her first full-time job, she found herself shrinking in the face of microaggressions and bias from colleagues and supervisors.

One day, after a particularly frustrating meeting where her ideas were dismissed and her expertise was questioned, Jada reached a breaking point. She knew that something needed to change if she was going to succeed and thrive in her career.

That's when Jada discovered the power of affirmations. She had heard about the practice before but always assumed it was too unscientific for her practical, analytical mind. But as she began researching the science behind affirmations and how they could boost confidence and performance, she decided to give it a try.

Jada started by writing down her biggest fears and doubts about her career, such as *"I'm not as qualified as my peers"* and *"I don't have what it takes to succeed in this industry."* Then, she crafted affirmations to counter each negative belief, such as *"I am highly skilled and deserving of my position"* and *"I have a unique perspective and value to bring to my work."*

Jada began repeating her affirmations every morning before work, as well as in moments of stress or self-doubt throughout the day. She also started keeping a small notebook on her desk with her affirmations written inside so she could easily reference them whenever needed.

As Jada continued her affirmation practice, she began to notice a shift in her mindset and behavior at work. Instead of staying quiet in meetings or downplaying her accomplishments, she started speaking up more confidently and owning her expertise. She stopped comparing herself to others and focused on her own unique strengths and contributions.

Jada also used affirmations to set ambitious goals and take bold actions toward her career growth. She affirmed her ability to learn new skills, take on challenging projects, and advocate for herself and her ideas. She began networking with other black women in tech, building a supportive community and finding mentors who could guide and encourage her along the way.

Over time, Jada's hard work and self-affirmation began to pay off. She was promoted to a leadership role within her department, and her innovative ideas were recognized and celebrated by colleagues and executives alike. She became known as a confident, competent leader who inspired and uplifted others, particularly other black women in the industry.

Today, Jada continues to use affirmations as a tool for personal and professional growth. She knows that the journey to success is never a straight line and that there will always be obstacles and setbacks along the way. But by affirming her own greatness and resilience, she has developed the mental strength and flexibility to navigate any challenge that comes her way.

Jada's story is a powerful example of how affirmations can help black women thrive in even the most challenging and competitive career environments. By affirming our skills, talents, and unique value, we develop the confidence and courage to go after our biggest dreams and make a meaningful impact in our fields.

If you find yourself struggling with self-doubt or imposter syndrome in your career, I encourage you to try incorporating affirmations into your daily routine. Start by identifying the negative beliefs or stories that may be holding you back, and craft affirmations that celebrate your strengths, accomplishments, and potential.

Remember that success is not just about external achievements but also about the internal growth and transformation that happens along the way. By affirming your own greatness and worth, you develop the resilience and adaptability to handle any obstacle or opportunity that comes your way. Trust in your own unique journey, and know that you have everything you need within you to create the career and life of your dreams.

8

AFFIRMATIONS FOR ABUNDANCE AND PROSPERITY

"The key to abundance is meeting limited circumstances with unlimited thoughts." - Marianne Williamson.

For centuries, black women have been the backbone of our families, communities, and economies, often working tirelessly to make ends meet and provide for loved ones. But despite our invaluable contributions, we have been systematically excluded from mainstream narratives of wealth, success, and prosperity. We have been taught to believe in scarcity, to accept less than we deserve, and to be grateful for whatever scraps come our way.

But the truth is, abundance is our birthright. We are the descendants of queens, warriors, and trailblazers who survived unimaginable hardships and created beauty, joy, and prosperity in the face of impossible odds. We carry within us the same resilience, creativity, and power that has sustained our ancestors for generations.

Affirmations are a powerful tool for tapping into this inner wealth and attracting more abundance and prosperity into our lives. By focusing our thoughts and energy on what we desire, rather than what we lack, we begin to shift our mindset from scarcity to sufficiency. We open ourselves up to new opportunities, resources, and relationships that align with our goals and values.

Research has shown that practicing gratitude and positive thinking can increase overall well-being, life satisfaction, and resilience (Wood et al., 2010). When we affirm the good in our lives, we train our brains to look for more of it, creating a virtuous cycle of abundance and appreciation.

Affirmations can also help us overcome limiting beliefs and fears around money, success, and worthiness. Many of us have internalized negative messages about our ability to achieve financial security or live an abundant life based on our race, gender, or socioeconomic status. By replacing these negative thoughts with empowering affirmations, we begin to see ourselves as capable, deserving, and fully supported by the universe.

HERE ARE SOME EXAMPLES OF AFFIRMATIONS FOR ABUNDANCE AND PROSPERITY:

- I am a magnet for abundance, success, and prosperity in all areas of my life.
- I trust in the universe's infinite supply and release any fears of lack or scarcity.
- I am grateful for the many blessings and opportunities that flow into my life every day.
- I am open to receiving wealth and abundance in expected and unexpected ways.
- I release any limiting beliefs or blocks around money and embrace a mindset of sufficiency.
- I am worthy of living a rich, fulfilling, and prosperous life, simply because I exist.
- I make wise, intuitive financial decisions that align with my values and goals.
- I celebrate others' success and know that there is more than enough to go around.

- I trust in my ability to manifest my dreams and desires through inspired action and faith.
- I am thankful for the abundance of love, joy, health, and prosperity in my life.

As you repeat these affirmations, take a moment to visualize yourself living a life of true abundance and prosperity. See yourself surrounded by beauty, comfort, and ease, with more than enough resources to share with others. Feel the deep sense of peace, gratitude, and fulfillment that comes from knowing you are always divinely supported and provided for.

Remember, abundance is about so much more than just financial wealth - it's about living a life of purpose, passion, and joy. It's about having meaningful relationships, experiences, and contributions that light you up from the inside out. It's about creating a legacy of love, service, and positive impact that will ripple out for generations to come.

In addition to affirmations, there are many other tools and practices that can support your journey to abundance and prosperity, such as:

- Cultivating a daily gratitude practice, such as keeping a gratitude journal or sharing your appreciation with others (Emmons & Stern, 2013)
- Creating a vision board or other visual representation of your goals and desires (Burton & Lent, 2016)
- Seeking out financial education and resources, such as books, podcasts, or workshops on budgeting, investing, and wealth-building (White, 2020)
- Practicing generosity and giving back to your community through volunteering, donating, or mentoring (Schervish, 2014)
- Celebrating your wins and milestones, no matter how big or small (Holden, 2015)

Remember, building a life of abundance and prosperity is a journey, not a destination. There may be challenges, setbacks, and detours along the way, but every step is an opportunity for growth, learning, and expansion. Trust in your own unique path and timeline, and don't compare yourself to others.

As the wise Oprah Winfrey once said, "*The greatest discovery of all time is that a person can change his future by merely changing his attitude.*" (Winfrey, 2014, p. 47)

By affirming your worthiness, strength, and limitless potential, you open yourself up to a world of abundance and prosperity beyond your wildest dreams. You become a shining example of what's possible for black women everywhere, inspiring others to claim their own birthright to joy, success, and fulfillment.

So take a deep breath, feel the unlimited abundance of the universe flowing through you, and repeat after me: I am a powerful creator of my reality. I attract wealth, prosperity, and abundance in all forms. I am open to receiving all the blessings and opportunities life has in store for me. And so it is.

"MANIFESTING ABUNDANCE: HOW AFFIRMATIONS TRANSFORMED MY RELATIONSHIP WITH MONEY"

Growing up in a low-income household, Maya always had a complicated relationship with money. She watched her single mother work multiple jobs just to keep food on the table and a roof over their heads and internalized the belief that money was scarce and hard to come by.

As Maya entered adulthood and started her own career, she found herself repeating the same patterns of financial struggle and insecurity. Despite working hard and earning a decent salary, she constantly worried about not having enough and often found herself living paycheck to paycheck.

One day, after a particularly stressful month of unexpected expenses and mounting debt, Maya decided that enough was enough. She knew that she needed to change her mindset and approach to money if she was ever going to break free from the cycle of lack and limitation.

That's when Maya discovered the power of affirmations and manifestation. She began researching the Law of Attraction and how thoughts and beliefs shape reality and became intrigued.

Maya started by identifying her biggest limiting beliefs around money, such as *"I will never have enough"* and *"Money is the root of all evil."* Then, she crafted affirmations to counter each negative belief, such as *"I am a magnet for abundance and prosperity"* and *"Money is a tool for creating positive change in the world."*

Maya began repeating her affirmations daily, both in the morning and before bed. She also started a manifestation journal, where she wrote down her financial goals and dreams as if they had already come true. She visualized herself living a life of abundance and ease, with more than enough money to support herself and her loved ones.

As Maya continued her affirmation and manifestation practice, she began to notice subtle shifts in her financial reality. Unexpected opportunities and windfalls started showing up, such as a surprise bonus at work or a generous gift from a friend. She also found herself making smarter financial decisions, such as creating a budget and saving for the future.

But the biggest transformation for Maya was in her own sense of worthiness and deserving. By affirming her right to abundance and prosperity, she began to release the shame and guilt she had carried around money for so long. She started to see herself as a powerful creator of her own financial reality rather than a victim of circumstance.

Over time, Maya's financial situation began to reflect her new, empowered mindset. She was able to pay off her debt, build a substantial savings account, and even start investing in her own business ventures. She became known as a generous and abundant person, always willing to share her resources and knowledge with others.

Today, Maya continues to use affirmations and manifestation as tools for creating a life of true prosperity and purpose. She knows that abundance is not just about material wealth but about living in alignment with her deepest values and desires. By affirming her worthiness and trusting in the universe's abundance, she has become a powerful force for positive change in her own life and in the world.

Maya's story is a reminder that our thoughts and beliefs about money have a profound impact on our financial reality. By using affirmations to shift our mindset from lack to abundance, we open ourselves up to new possibilities and opportunities for prosperity.

If you find yourself struggling with financial insecurity or limitation, I encourage you to try incorporating affirmations and manifestation into your daily practice. Start by identifying the negative beliefs or stories you may be holding around money and craft affirmations that affirm your right to abundance, prosperity, and financial freedom.

Remember that true wealth is not just about the numbers in your bank account but about the richness of your experiences, relationships, and contributions to the world. By affirming your worthiness and value, you attract the resources and opportunities you need to live a life of purpose, passion, and plenty. Trust in the universe's abundance, and know that you are always supported and provided for.

9

AFFIRMATIONS FOR SELF-CONFIDENCE AND EMPOWERMENT

"Our deepest fear is not that we are inadequate. Our deepest fear is that we are powerful beyond measure." - Marianne Williamson.

As black women, we are often taught to shrink ourselves, to play small, and to doubt our own power and potential. From a young age, we may internalize messages that we are not smart enough, talented enough, or deserving enough to chase our biggest dreams and make a meaningful impact in the world.

But the truth is, we are born with an inherent sense of worth, creativity, and resilience that cannot be diminished by external circumstances or opinions. We are the descendants of people who have defied impossible odds and shattered glass ceilings throughout history. We carry within us the same courage, brilliance, and unstoppable spirit that has fueled movements, built empires, and transformed the world.

Affirmations are a powerful tool for reconnecting with this inner strength and confidence, especially in moments of doubt, fear, or uncertainty. By focusing our thoughts and energy on our unique gifts, talents, and contributions, we train our brains to see ourselves through a lens of empowerment and possibility. We become more resilient in the face of challenges, more assertive in advocating for our needs and boundaries, and more confident in pursuing our passions and purpose.

Research has shown that self-affirmation can boost self-esteem, reduce stress and anxiety, and improve overall well-being (Cohen & Sherman, 2014). When we affirm our inherent worth and value, we become less reactive to external validation or criticism and more grounded in our own sense of self. We develop a deep trust in our own judgment, intuition, and abilities, even in the face of doubt or adversity.

Affirmations can also help us rewrite limiting stories and beliefs that may be holding us back from reaching our full potential. Many of us have internalized negative messages about our intelligence, beauty, or capabilities based on our race, gender, or background. By replacing these disempowering thoughts with empowering affirmations, we begin to see ourselves in a new light – as the brilliant, capable, and unstoppable forces we truly are.

HERE ARE SOME EXAMPLES OF AFFIRMATIONS FOR SELF-CONFIDENCE AND EMPOWERMENT:

- I am a powerful, confident, and capable woman worthy of love, respect, and success.
- I trust my intuition and make decisions that align with my highest good.
- I embrace my unique talents, gifts, and quirks, knowing that they are my superpowers.
- I am resilient and can handle any challenge that comes my way with grace and strength.
- I speak my truth with clarity, conviction, and compassion, even when my voice shakes.

- I am not defined by my mistakes or setbacks but by my ability to learn, grow, and keep moving forward.
- I surround myself with people who see my brilliance, challenge me to grow, and support me unconditionally.
- I am grateful for my mind, body, and spirit, and I treat myself with kindness and respect.
- I am open to new opportunities, experiences, and adventures that stretch me beyond my comfort zone.
- I am a force for positive change in my life, my community, and the world.

As you repeat these affirmations, take a moment to visualize yourself embodying the qualities of confidence, courage, and empowerment. See yourself standing tall, speaking your truth, and taking bold action towards your dreams. Feel the unshakeable sense of self-assurance and trust that comes from knowing you are divinely guided and supported at all times.

Remember, building self-confidence and empowerment is an ongoing journey, not a one-time event. There may be moments when old fears, doubts, or insecurities resurface, especially when you're stepping outside your comfort zone or trying something new. This is completely normal and natural. The key is to meet these moments with compassion, curiosity, and a commitment to your own growth and healing.

In addition to affirmations, there are many other tools and practices that can support your journey to greater self-confidence and empowerment, such as:

- Setting healthy boundaries and learning to say "no" when something doesn't align with your values or priorities (Brown, 2018)
- Practicing self-care and prioritizing activities that nourish your mind, body, and spirit (Bryant-Davis et al., 2017)
- Seeking out mentors, role models, and supportive

- communities who can offer guidance, encouragement, and accountability (Thomas et al., 2020)
- Challenging negative self-talk and reframing failures as opportunities for growth and learning (Dweck, 2006)
- Celebrating your wins, milestones, and accomplishments, no matter how big or small (Duckworth, 2016)

Remember, your worth is not something you have to earn or prove – it is an inherent part of who you are. You are enough, exactly as you are, and you have everything you need within you to create a life of purpose, passion, and impact.

As the phenomenal Maya Angelou once said, *"You may write me down in history / With your bitter, twisted lies, / You may trod me in the very dirt / But still, like dust, I'll rise."* (Angelou, 1978)

By affirming your power, brilliance, and resilience, you become an unstoppable force for change in your own life and in the world around you. You inspire others to rise up, speak out, and claim their own greatness. You become a living testament to the unshakable strength and spirit of black women everywhere.

So take a deep breath, feel the fire of your own power and potential burning within you, and repeat after me: I am a confident, courageous, and unstoppable force. I trust in my abilities, my journey, and my purpose. I am ready to shine my light and make a positive impact in the world. And so it is.

"CLAIMING MY POWER: HOW AFFIRMATIONS HELPED ME RISE ABOVE CHALLENGES"

A few years ago, I found myself in a deep crisis of confidence. After a series of personal and professional setbacks, including a difficult breakup and a job loss, I felt like I had lost my sense of purpose and direction in life. I questioned my own worth and abilities and struggled with feelings of anxiety, depression, and self-doubt.

As a high achiever and a natural leader, I have always prided myself on my ability to handle challenges and overcome obstacles. But this time, I felt like I had hit a wall. I didn't know how to move forward or reclaim my sense of power and agency in my own life.

That's when I turned to affirmations. I had used affirmations before, but more as a superficial pick-me-up than a deep practice. But as I began researching the neuroscience behind affirmations and how they could rewire the brain for greater resilience and self-belief, I decided to commit to the practice in a more intentional way.

I started by writing down my biggest fears and doubts, such as *"I am not good enough"* and *"I will never achieve my dreams."* Then, I crafted affirmations to counter each negative belief, such as *"I am more than enough, just as I am"* and *"I trust in my ability to create the life I desire."*

I began repeating my affirmations every morning and evening, as well as in moments of stress or self-doubt throughout the day. I also started a daily practice of meditation and journaling, using my affirmations as a guide for self-reflection and goal-setting.

As I continued my affirmation practice, I began to notice a shift in my mindset and energy. Instead of dwelling on my failures and limitations, I started focusing on my strengths and opportunities for growth. I became more proactive in seeking out new challenges and learning experiences rather than shying away from them out of fear.

One of the most powerful moments in my affirmation journey came when I was offered a new job opportunity that initially seemed beyond my reach. It was a leadership role in a field I had always been passionate about, but I doubted my qualifications and experience. My initial instinct was to talk myself out of even applying, but then I remembered one of my affirmations: "I am capable of achieving anything I set my mind to."

With that affirmation in mind, I took a leap of faith and applied for the job. To my surprise and delight, I was offered the position, and it turned out to be one of the most rewarding and fulfilling experiences of my career. By claiming my own power and potential through affirmations, I opened myself up to new possibilities and opportunities that I never would have imagined before.

Today, I continue to use affirmations as a daily practice for self-empowerment and growth. I know that challenges and setbacks are inevitable, but I also know that I have the inner strength and resilience to rise above them. By affirming my own worth, abilities, and potential, I have developed a deep trust in myself and my journey, even when the path ahead is uncertain.

My affirmation journey has taught me that true power comes from within. It is not about external validation or achievement, but about claiming our own inherent worth and potential as individuals. When we affirm our own greatness and trust in our ability to overcome challenges, we become unstoppable forces for positive change in our own lives and in the world.

If you find yourself facing a crisis of confidence or a seemingly insurmountable obstacle, I encourage you to try incorporating affirmations into your daily practice. Start by identifying the negative beliefs or stories that may be holding you back, and craft affirmations that celebrate your strengths, resilience, and potential.

Remember that growth and transformation are not always easy or comfortable, but they are always worth it. By claiming your own power and trusting in your journey, you open yourself up to a world of endless possibilities and opportunities. Know that you are stronger than you realize and that you have everything you need within you to rise above any challenge that comes your way.

CONCLUSION: EMBRACING YOUR AFFIRMED SELF - A LIFELONG JOURNEY

"Affirm the power, beauty, and rightness of who you are. The world cannot contradict you." - Iyanla Vanzant.

As we come to the end of our journey through the transformative power of affirmations, it's important to remember that this is not truly an ending, but a beginning. The work of self-affirmation, self-love, and empowerment is a lifelong practice - one that requires patience, dedication, and compassion for yourself.

Throughout this book, we've explored how affirmations can impact various aspects of our lives as black women - from healing and self-love to career success and financial abundance. We've delved into the science behind affirmations, shared personal stories of transformation, and provided practical tools for incorporating affirmations into your daily life.

Now, as you prepare to continue this journey beyond these pages, here are some key takeaways and actionable steps to help you fully embrace your affirmed self:

1. Consistency is Key: Like any new habit, the practice of affirmations requires consistency to truly take root in your subconscious mind. Commit to a daily affirmation practice, even if it's just for a few minutes each day. Remember, small, consistent efforts can lead to profound changes over time.
2. Personalize Your Affirmations: While the affirmations provided in this book can be powerful tools, don't be afraid to create your own. The most effective affirmations are those that resonate deeply with your personal experiences, goals, and values. Take time to reflect on what you truly want to affirm in your life and craft statements that speak directly to those desires.
3. Address Resistance with Compassion: It's normal to experience resistance or disbelief when you first start working with affirmations, especially if they contradict long-held negative beliefs. When this happens, don't judge or criticize yourself. Instead, approach the resistance with curiosity and compassion. Ask yourself where the doubt is coming from and if it's serving your highest good.
4. Combine Affirmations with Action: While affirmations can shift your mindset and beliefs, it's important to pair them with aligned action. If you're affirming career success, for example, make sure you're also taking practical steps towards your professional goals. The combination of positive thinking and positive action is where true transformation occurs.
5. Create an Affirmation-Rich Environment: Surround yourself with reminders of your affirmations. This could be through post-it notes on your mirror, a vision board in your office, or affirmation apps on your phone. The more you immerse yourself in positive, empowering messages, the more natural they'll become to your way of thinking.
6. Share Your Journey: Consider starting an affirmation circle with friends or joining online communities focused on personal growth and empowerment. Sharing your experiences, challenges, and successes can provide

accountability, support, and inspiration as you continue your affirmation practice.
7. Celebrate Your Progress: Take time to acknowledge and celebrate the positive changes you notice in your life, no matter how small they may seem. Each moment of increased confidence, each brave decision, each step towards your goals is worthy of celebration.
8. Stay Open to Growth: As you evolve and grow, your affirmations may need to evolve too. Regularly check in with yourself to ensure your affirmations still align with your current goals and desires. Don't be afraid to update or change your affirmations as needed.
9. Trust the Process: Remember that change and growth are not always linear processes. There may be times when you feel like you're taking two steps forward and one step back. Trust in the power of your affirmations and in your own resilience. Every experience, even the challenging ones, is an opportunity for growth and learning.
10. Extend Compassion to Others: As you cultivate greater self-love and empowerment through affirmations, extend that same compassion and support to other black women in your life. By lifting each other up, we create a ripple effect of positivity and empowerment that can transform our communities and the world.

In closing, I want to remind you of a powerful truth: You are worthy of love, success, abundance, and joy simply because you exist. Your worth is not determined by your achievements, your relationships, or your possessions. It is inherent, unshakeable, and infinite.

As you continue on your journey of self-affirmation and empowerment, know that you carry within you the strength, wisdom, and resilience of generations of black women who came before you. Their dreams and sacrifices have paved the way for you to stand tall in your power and claim the life you desire and deserve.

So go forth, beautiful soul. Affirm your worth, speak your truth, and shine your light brightly. The world is waiting for the unique magic that only you can bring. Remember always:

- I am powerful beyond measure.
- I am worthy of all good things.
- I am enough, just as i am.
- and so it is.

A CALL TO ACTION: SHARE YOUR LIGHT

"You are not just here in this world to exist, you are here to make a difference." - Dr. Cindy Trimm.

Beloved reader,

If you've almost made it to the end of this book, congratulations! You have taken a powerful step towards affirming your inherent worth, beauty, and potential as a black woman. I am so grateful to have been a part of your journey and to have witnessed your growth and transformation along the way.

As we come to the close of our time together, I have one final request: please take a moment to leave an honest review of this book and share your experience with others. Your words have the power to inspire, encourage, and uplift other black women who may be struggling with similar doubts, fears, or challenges.

By leaving a review, you are not only supporting the mission and message of this book - you are also claiming your voice and your power as a force for positive change. You never know who may read your words and find the courage and inspiration they need to start their own journey of self-love and empowerment.

Remember, affirming our worth and changing our lives is not a solo endeavor - it is a collective one. When we come together as a community to support, celebrate, and uplift one another, there is no limit to what we can achieve. Your review is a vital part of that collective movement towards healing, justice, and liberation.

So please, take a few moments to reflect on your experience with this book and share your honest thoughts and insights. Whether you found it life-changing, thought-provoking, or simply enjoyable, your perspective matters and deserves to be heard.

To leave a review, simply scan the QR code:

Thank you again for being a part of this journey with me. I am so honored to have had the opportunity to affirm your greatness and witness your unfolding. Keep shining your light, keep speaking your truth, and keep affirming your endless potential. The world needs your magic now more than ever.

With love, gratitude, and immense faith in you,

Imani Elkins

AFFIRMATION JOURNAL SECTION

How I feel after repeating this affirmation:

One small action I can take today to align with this affirmation:

Monthly Progress Tracker

At the end of each month, reflect on your affirmation practice:

Month: _____

1. What positive changes have I noticed in my thoughts or behaviors?
2. Which affirmations resonated with me the most?
3. What challenges did I face in my affirmation practice?
4. How can I deepen my practice next month?

Remember, your affirmation journey is unique to you. Be patient and compassionate with yourself as you grow and evolve. You are doing important, transformative work!

BIBLIOGRAPHY

Angelou, M. (1978). *And still I rise*. New York, NY: Random House.
Arruda, W. (2019). *Digital you: Real personal branding in the virtual age*. New York, NY: McGraw-Hill.
Brown, B. (2018). *Dare to lead: Brave work. Tough conversations. Whole hearts*. New York, NY: Random House.
Bryant-Davis, T. (2013). Sister friends: A reflection and analysis of the therapeutic role of sisterhood in African American women's lives. *Women & Therapy, 36*(1-2), 110-120.
Bryant-Davis, T., Ullman, S. E., Tsong, Y., Anderson, G., Counts, P., Tillman, S., ... & Gray, A. (2017). Healing pathways: Longitudinal effects of religious coping and social support on PTSD symptoms in African American sexual assault survivors. *Journal of Trauma & Dissociation, 18*(1), 114-128.
Burton, L. M., & Lent, J. (2016). The use of vision boards as a therapeutic intervention. *Journal of Creativity in Mental Health, 11*(1), 52-65.
Cohen, G. L., & Sherman, D. K. (2014). The psychology of change: Self-affirmation and social psychological intervention. *Annual Review of Psychology, 65*, 333-371.
Combs, G. M. (2003). The duality of race and gender for managerial African American women: Implications of informal social networks on career advancement. *Human Resource Development Review, 2*(4), 385-405.
Creswell, J. D., Dutcher, J. M., Klein, W. M., Harris, P. R., & Levine, J. M. (2013). Self-affirmation improves problem-solving under stress. *PLoS One, 8*(5), e62593.
Davis, D. D. (2016). The journey to the top: Stories on the intersection of race and gender for African American women in academia and business. *Journal of Research Initiatives, 2*(1), 4.
Duckworth, A. (2016). *Grit: The power of passion and perseverance*. New York, NY: Scribner.
Dweck, C. S. (2006). *Mindset: The new psychology of success*. New York, NY: Random House.
Dweck, C. S. (2016). What having a "growth mindset" actually means. *Harvard Business Review, 13*, 213-226.
Emmons, R. A., & Stern, R. (2013). Gratitude as a psychotherapeutic intervention. *Journal of Clinical Psychology, 69*(8), 846-855.
Holden, K. (2015). What helps you keep going? Black women's wisdom on staying resilient across the life span. *Journal of Black Psychology, 41*(5), 424-444.
Johnson, H. D., Phelps, T., & Delongchamp, R. R. (2019). Affirmations and somatic experiencing in the treatment of African American trauma survivors. *Journal of Black Psychology, 45*(1), 3-28.
Kelly, S., Jeremie-Brink, G., & Smith, W. A. (2018). African American couples: Socio-

cultural factors impacting marriage and health. *Journal of Black Sexuality and Relationships, 5*(1), 1-22.

Martens, A., Johns, M., Greenberg, J., & Schimel, J. (2006). Combating stereotype threat: The effect of self-affirmation on women's intellectual performance. *Journal of Experimental Social Psychology, 42*(2), 236-243.

Neal-Barnett, A. M., Stadulis, R., Murray, M., Payne, M. R., Thomas, A., & Salley, B. B. (2011). Sister circles as a culturally relevant intervention for anxious Black women. *Clinical Psychology: Science and Practice, 18*(3), 266-273.

Obama, M. (2018). Becoming. Crown Publishing Group.

Robbins, M. (2017). The 5 Second Rule: Transform your Life, Work, and Confidence with Everyday Courage. Savio Republic.

Roberson, Q. M. (2006). Disentangling the meanings of diversity and inclusion in organizations. *Group & Organization Management, 31*(2), 212-236.

Rosenberg, M. B. (2015). *Nonviolent communication: A language of life* (3rd ed.). Encinitas, CA: PuddleDancer Press.

Schervish, P. G. (2014). Major donors, major motives: The people and purposes behind major gifts. *New Directions for Philanthropic Fundraising, 2014*(47), 59-87.

Sherman, D. K., & Cohen, G. L. (2006). The psychology of self-defense: Self-affirmation theory. *Advances in Experimental Social Psychology, 38*, 183-242.

Sherman, D. K., Hartson, K. A., Binning, K. R., Purdie-Vaughns, V., Garcia, J., Taborsky-Barba, S., ... & Cohen, G. L. (2013). Deflecting the trajectory and changing the narrative: How self-affirmation affects academic performance and motivation under identity threat. *Journal of Personality and Social Psychology, 104*(4), 591.

Sherman, K. A., Przezdziecki, A., Alcorso, J., Kilby, C. J., Elder, E., Boyages, J., ... & Mackie, H. (2017). Reducing body image–related distress in women with breast cancer using a structured online writing exercise: Results from the My Changed Body randomized controlled trial. *Journal of Clinical Oncology, 36*(19), 1930-1940.

Stuckey, H. L., & Nobel, J. (2010). The connection between art, healing, and public health: A review of current literature. *American Journal of Public Health, 100*(2), 254-263.

Thomas, A., Moss-Racusin, C., & Sanzari, C. (2020). Mentorship, intersectionality, and the road less traveled. *Industrial and Organizational Psychology, 13*(4), 561-565.

Trimm, C. (2015). The 40 Day Soul Fast: Your Journey to Authentic Living. Destiny Image Publishers.

White, A. M. (2020). Disrupting the master narrative: Teaching and learning through a Black feminist framework. *Equity & Excellence in Education, 53*(4), 495-506.

Winfrey, O. (2014). *What I know for sure*. New York, NY: Flatiron Books.

Wood, A. M., Froh, J. J., & Geraghty, A. W. (2010). Gratitude and well-being: A review and theoretical integration. *Clinical Psychology Review, 30*(7), 890-905.

1865 POSITIVE AFFIRMATIONS
FOR
BLACK WOMEN

A Comprehensive List of Over 1,000 Affirmations You Can Read or Listen to Anytime, Anywhere

IMANI ELKINS

To the extraordinary black women who have touched my life with their unwavering strength, boundless resilience, and unconditional love - and to every black woman who needs a reminder of her inherent power, beauty, and worth, I dedicate this book to you. May these affirmations be a guiding light on your path to self-discovery, healing, and transformation.

INTRODUCTION

"You yourself, as much as anybody in the entire universe, deserve your love and affection." - Buddha.

Welcome to "1865 Positive Affirmations for Black Women" - a book dedicated to empowering and uplifting you on your journey to a more fulfilling life. The number 1865 holds deep historical and symbolic significance for black women in America. It was the year that the 13th Amendment was ratified, officially abolishing slavery in the United States (National Archives, 2022). This marked a pivotal turning point in the long and painful struggle for freedom, equality, and human dignity.

1865 represents the resilience, strength, and unbreakable spirit of our ancestors who endured unspeakable horrors and fought tirelessly for the right to live as free, autonomous beings. It reminds us that even in the face of the most unimaginable adversity, we have the power within us to rise up, break chains, and forge a new path for ourselves and future generations.

By naming this book "1865 Positive Affirmations," we honor the legacy of those who came before us and draw strength from their courage and determination. We acknowledge that though the wounds of slavery and oppression still linger, we are not defined by our pain but by our potential to heal, grow, and thrive. 1865 is not just a number - it is a powerful invocation of our inherent right to freedom, respect, and self-actualization.

As black women today, we continue to face unique challenges and pressures. From the workplace to our relationships and inner lives, it can be difficult to maintain a sense of confidence, self-worth, and joy (hooks, 2000). But within each of us lies the same indomitable spirit that carried our ancestors through the darkest of times (Walker, 1983).

This book demonstrates the power of affirming our worth, wisdom, and strength. Each of the 1865 affirmations within these pages is a reminder of the incredible reservoir of strength, beauty, and potential that resides within you. They are a tool for liberating yourself from limiting beliefs, healing deep-seated wounds, and stepping into the glorious fullness of who you were always meant to be.

As you embark on this journey of self-discovery and transformation, know that you carry the hopes and dreams of generations of black women who fought for the freedoms you now enjoy. Honor their sacrifice by daring to live boldly, love fiercely, and pursue your passions unapologetically.

You are the embodiment of your ancestors' resilience and strength. 1865 is your birthright, your rallying cry, your north star. Wear it as a badge of honor, a reminder of how far you've come and how far you have yet to go. Let it be the fire that propels you forward, the light that illuminates your path, the foundation upon which you build your queendom.

This book is designed to be a powerful tool in your affirmation practice, providing you with a comprehensive list of affirmations that you can read or listen to anytime, anywhere. Whether you're driving to work, exercising, or simply relaxing at home, these affirmations are here to uplift, empower, and inspire you on your journey of self-discovery and transformation.

Welcome to 1865, beautiful. Your freedom awaits.

With love and solidarity,

Imani

1

AFFIRMATIONS 1 - 250

"What you get by achieving your goals is not as important as what you become by achieving your goals." - Ziglar.

1.
I am worthy of love, respect, and appreciation.

2.
I trust my inner wisdom and intuition.

3.
I am capable of achieving my goals.

4.
I embrace self-compassion and release negative self-talk.

5.
I am grateful for my unique talents and qualities.

6.
I deserve success, happiness, and fulfillment.

7.
I focus on the positive aspects of my life.

8.
I am confident, competent, and capable.

9.
I am surrounded by love and support.

10.
I am resilient and can overcome challenges.

11.
I prioritize my own time, energy, and attention.

12.
I trust in my life's journey.

13.
I am open to abundance in all areas of my life.

14.
I release limiting beliefs and embrace my full potential.

15.
I am grateful for my body, and all it does for me.

16.
I create my reality with intention and purpose.

17.
I choose to see the beauty in myself and others.

18.
I deserve healthy, loving relationships.

19.
I am successful in my career and financial endeavors.

20.
I am at peace with myself and my life.

21.
I am a positive influence on those around me.

22.
I am constantly learning and growing.

23.
I am worthy of respect and admiration.

24.
I deserve joy, laughter, and happiness.

25.
I embrace my uniqueness and individuality.

26.
I am grateful for the lessons and experiences in my life.

27.
I attract positive opportunities and experiences.

28.
I am worthy of forgiveness and second chances.

29.
I trust in the power of my dreams and aspirations.

30.
I am capable of healing and releasing the past.

31.
I am surrounded by abundance and prosperity.

32.
I focus on solutions, not problems.

33.
I am grateful for my strength and resilience.

34.
I am open to receiving love and support from others.

35.
I am capable of creating positive change in my life.

36.
I deserve a life filled with purpose and meaning.

37.
I trust in the timing and unfolding of my journey.

38.
I am a powerful force for good in the world.

39.
I celebrate my successes, no matter how small.

40.
I am grateful for the people in my life who support and inspire me.

41.
I am capable of overcoming any fear or obstacle.

42.
I deserve a life filled with adventure and excitement.

43.
I trust in my ability to make wise decisions.

44.
I am surrounded by opportunities for growth and learning.

45.
I let go of comparison and embrace my own path.

46.
I am grateful for my intelligence and creativity.

47.
I am open to receiving guidance and support from the universe.

48.
I am capable of achieving a healthy work-life balance.

49.
I deserve a fulfilling and passionate relationship.

50.
I trust in my ability to communicate my needs and desires.

51.
I am surrounded by beauty and miracles every day.

52.
I focus on the present moment and find joy in it.

53.
I am grateful for my intuition and inner guidance.

54.
I am open to new experiences and adventures.

55.
I am capable of creating a life filled with joy and laughter.

56.
I deserve financial abundance and security.

57.
I trust in my ability to adapt and grow through challenges.

58.
I am a valuable member of my community and the world.

59.
I release any guilt or shame that holds me back.

60.
I am grateful for the love and compassion I have for myself.

61.
I am open to receiving the support and resources I need.

62.
I am capable of building a strong and empowered mindset.

63.
I deserve a life filled with peace and harmony.

64.
I trust in the divine timing of my life's events.

65.
I am surrounded by positive and uplifting influences.

66.
I embrace change and welcome new beginnings.

67.
I am grateful for the challenges that help me grow and evolve.

68.
I am open to healing my past and creating a brighter future.

69.
I am capable of achieving my goals and dreams.

70.
I deserve deep, restful sleep and rejuvenation.

71.
I trust in my ability to create healthy boundaries.

72.
I am surrounded by people who value and appreciate me.

73.
I choose to see the world through the lens of love and compassion.

74.
I am grateful for the strength and resilience of my ancestors.

75.
I am open to receiving abundance in all forms.

76.
I am capable of creating a life filled with purpose and impact.

77.
I deserve a healthy, nourished body.

78.
I trust in my ability to overcome any setback or disappointment.

79.
I am surrounded by opportunities for success and growth.

80.
I embrace my femininity and womanhood.

81.
I am grateful for the wisdom and knowledge I possess.

82.
I am open to receiving love and appreciation from myself and others.

83.
I am capable of creating a life filled with passion and excitement.

84.
I deserve a career that aligns with my values and purpose.

85.
I trust in my ability to set and achieve my goals.

86.
I am surrounded by positivity and good fortune.

87.
I let go of any self-doubt or insecurity.

88.
I am grateful for the unique gifts and talents I have to share with the world.

89.
I am open to receiving guidance and mentorship from those I admire.

90.
I am capable of building a strong and empowered financial future.

91.
I deserve a life filled with love, laughter, and joy.

92.
I trust in my ability to make a positive difference in the world.

93.
I am surrounded by an abundance of opportunities and resources.

94.
I embrace my natural beauty and radiance.

95.
I am grateful for the love and support of my family and friends.

96.
I am open to receiving recognition and praise for my accomplishments.

97.
I am capable of creating a life filled with adventure and exploration.

98.
I deserve a loving, supportive partnership.

99.
I trust in my ability to heal and release any past traumas.

100.
I am surrounded by positivity and good vibes.

101.
I am capable of creating a life filled with joy, ease, and flow.

102.
I deserve a life that exceeds my wildest dreams.

103.
I trust in my ability to handle anything that comes my way.

104.
I am surrounded by positive, supportive, and uplifting people.

105.
I embrace my quirks, flaws, and imperfections.

106.
I am grateful for the abundance and prosperity I experience.

107.
I am open to receiving new opportunities for adventure and exploration.

108.
I am capable of creating a life filled with passion, purpose, and joy.

109.
I deserve deep, meaningful connections with others.

110.
I trust in my ability to make positive, healthy choices for myself.

111.
I am surrounded by an abundance of love, joy, and positivity.

112.
I let go of any negative self-talk or criticism.

113.
I am grateful for the strength and resilience I have developed.

114.
I am open to receiving guidance and support from my intuition.

115.
I am capable of building a successful, thriving career.

116.
I deserve a life filled with abundance, prosperity, and wealth.

117.
I trust in my ability to create a life that aligns with my values and beliefs.

118.
I am surrounded by opportunities for growth, learning, and development.

119.
I embrace my unique personality and quirks.

120.
I am grateful for the love and appreciation I have for myself.

121.
I am open to receiving new ideas and perspectives.

122.
I am capable of creating a life filled with harmony, balance, and peace.

123.
I deserve a life filled with excitement, adventure, and fun.

124.
I trust in my ability to overcome any challenge or obstacle.

125.
I am surrounded by an abundance of happiness, laughter, and joy.

126.

I let go of any limiting beliefs or self-doubt.

127.
I am grateful for the positive impact I have on those around me.

128.
I am open to receiving love, support, and encouragement from others.

129.
I am capable of building a life filled with purpose, meaning, and fulfillment.

130.
I deserve a life filled with passion, romance, and intimacy.

131.
I trust in my ability to create a life that brings me joy and satisfaction.

132.
I am surrounded by an abundance of creativity, inspiration, and innovation.

133.
I embrace my divine feminine energy and power.

134.
I am grateful for the courage and confidence I possess.

135.
I am open to receiving new opportunities for success and achievement.

136.
I am capable of creating a life filled with love, compassion, and kindness.

137.
I deserve a life filled with joy, happiness, and positivity.

138.
I trust in my ability to create a life that is authentic and true to myself.

139.
I am surrounded by an abundance of peace, calm, and tranquility.

140.
I let go of any past mistakes, regrets, or failures.

141.
I am grateful for the wisdom and knowledge I have gained through my experiences.

142.
I am open to receiving new opportunities for healing and transformation.

143.
I am capable of building a life filled with grace, ease, and flow.

144.
I deserve a life filled with beauty, wonder, and magic.

145.
I trust in my ability to create a life that is rich, fulfilling, and rewarding.

146.
I am surrounded by an abundance of opportunities, possibilities, and potential.

147.
I embrace my unique gifts, talents, and abilities.

148.
I am grateful for the love and support I receive from the universe.

149.
I am open to receiving new opportunities for love, joy, and happiness.

150.
I am capable of creating a life filled with abundance, prosperity, and success.

151.
I deserve a life filled with peace, harmony, and balance.

152.
I trust in my ability to create a life that is full of purpose and meaning.

153.
I am surrounded by an abundance of positive energy, vibrations, and frequencies.

154.
I let go of any fear, anxiety, or worry.

155.
I am grateful for the strength and resilience of my mind, body, and spirit.

156.
I am open to receiving new opportunities for growth, expansion, and abundance.

157.
I am capable of creating a life filled with joy, positivity, and optimism.

158.
I deserve a life filled with love, compassion, and understanding.

159.
I trust in my ability to create a life that is authentic, genuine, and real.

160.
I am surrounded by an abundance of motivation, inspiration, and encouragement.

161.
I embrace my unique journey and path in life.

162.
I am grateful for the opportunities and blessings that come my way.

163.
I am open to receiving new insights, ideas, and revelations.

164.
I am capable of building a life filled with success, achievement, and accomplishment.

165.
I deserve a life filled with happiness, contentment, and satisfaction.

166.
I trust in my ability to create a life that is rich in love, laughter, and joy.

167.
I am surrounded by an abundance of positivity, enthusiasm, and excitement.

168.
I let go of any self-limiting beliefs or thoughts.

169.

I am grateful for the love and appreciation I have for my body and mind.

170.
I am open to receiving new opportunities for self-discovery and personal growth.

171.
I am capable of creating a life filled with passion, purpose, and meaning.

172.
I deserve a life filled with abundance, prosperity, and wealth.

173.
I trust in my ability to create a life that aligns with my values and beliefs.

174.
I am surrounded by an abundance of creativity, innovation, and inspiration.

175.
I embrace my unique talents, skills, and abilities.

176.
I am grateful for the positive relationships and connections in my life.

177.
I am open to receiving new opportunities for love, romance, and intimacy.

178.
I am capable of building a life filled with success, prosperity, and abundance.

179.
I deserve a life filled with joy, peace, and happiness.

180.
I trust in my ability to create a life that is meaningful, fulfilling, and rewarding.

181.
I am surrounded by an abundance of love, light, and positivity.

182.
I let go of any negative thoughts, emotions, or beliefs.

183.
I am grateful for the strength, courage, and resilience I possess.

184.
I am open to receiving new opportunities for healing, growth, and transformation.

185.
I am capable of creating a life filled with purpose, passion, and joy.

186.
I deserve a life filled with love, happiness, and fulfillment.

187.
I trust in my ability to create a life that is rich in love, laughter, and happiness.

188.
I am surrounded by an abundance of peace, calm, and tranquility.

189.
I embrace my natural beauty and radiance.

190.
I am grateful for the wisdom and knowledge I possess.

191.
I am open to receiving recognition and praise for my accomplishments.

192.
I am capable of creating a life filled with adventure and exploration.

193.
I deserve a strong, healthy body that carries me through life.

194.
I trust in my ability to attract positive people and experiences.

195.
I am surrounded by an abundance of love and support.

196.
I embrace my sensuality and sexual energy.

197.
I am grateful for the courage and bravery I possess.

198.
I am open to receiving new opportunities for growth and expansion.

199.
I am capable of creating a life filled with freedom and flexibility.

200.
I deserve respect, admiration, and appreciation.

201.

I trust in my ability to communicate my thoughts and ideas effectively.

202.
I am surrounded by beauty, wonder, and miracles.

203.
I let go of any fear or worry about the future.

204.
I am grateful for the peace and calm I am able to cultivate within.

205.
I am open to receiving new opportunities for adventure and exploration.

206.
I am capable of building a life filled with joy, ease, and flow.

207.
I deserve a life that exceeds my wildest dreams.

208.
I trust in my ability to handle anything that comes my way.

209.
I am surrounded by positive, supportive, and uplifting people.

210.
I embrace my quirks, flaws, and imperfections.

211.
I am grateful for the abundance and prosperity I experience.

212.

I am open to receiving new opportunities for passion, purpose, and joy.

213.
I am capable of creating a life filled with deep, meaningful connections.

214.
I deserve positive, healthy choices for myself.

215.
I trust in my ability to create an abundance of love, joy, and positivity.

216.
I am surrounded by opportunities for growth, learning, and development.

217.
I let go of any negative self-talk or criticism.

218.
I am grateful for the strength and resilience I have developed.

219.
I am open to receiving guidance and support from my intuition.

220.
I am capable of building a successful, thriving career.

221.
I deserve a life filled with abundance, prosperity, and wealth.

222.
I trust in my ability to create a life that aligns with my values and beliefs.

223.
I am surrounded by an abundance of happiness, laughter, and joy.

224.
I embrace my unique personality and quirks.

225.
I am grateful for the love and appreciation I have for myself.

226.
I am open to receiving new ideas and perspectives.

227.
I am capable of creating a life filled with harmony, balance, and peace.

228.
I deserve a life filled with excitement, adventure, and fun.

229.
I trust in my ability to overcome any challenge or obstacle.

230.
I am surrounded by an abundance of creativity, inspiration, and innovation.

231.
I let go of any limiting beliefs or self-doubt.

232.
I am grateful for the positive impact I have on those around me.

233.
I am open to receiving love, support, and encouragement from others.

234.

I am capable of building a life filled with purpose, meaning, and fulfillment.

235.
I deserve a life filled with passion, romance, and intimacy.

236.
I trust in my ability to create a life that brings me joy and satisfaction.

237.
I am surrounded by an abundance of peace, calm, and tranquility.

238.
I embrace my divine feminine energy and power.

239.
I am grateful for the courage and confidence I possess.

240.
I am open to receiving new opportunities for success and achievement.

241.
I am capable of creating a life filled with love, compassion, and kindness.

242.
I deserve a life filled with joy, happiness, and positivity.

243.
I trust in my ability to create a life that is authentic and true to myself.

244.
I am surrounded by an abundance of motivation, inspiration, and encouragement.

245.
I let go of any past mistakes, regrets, or failures.

246.
I am grateful for the wisdom and knowledge I have gained through my experiences.

247.
I am open to receiving new opportunities for healing and transformation.

248.
I am capable of building a life filled with grace, ease, and flow.

249.
I deserve a life filled with beauty, wonder, and magic.

250.
I trust in my ability to create a life that is rich, fulfilling, and rewarding.

2

AFFIRMATIONS 251 - 500

"The only limit to our realization of tomorrow is our doubts of today." - Roosevelt.

251.
I am surrounded by an abundance of opportunities, possibilities, and potential.

252.
I embrace my unique gifts, talents, and abilities.

253.
I am grateful for the love and support I receive from the universe.

254.
I am open to receiving new opportunities for love, joy, and happiness.

255.
I am capable of creating a life filled with abundance, prosperity, and success.

256.
I deserve a life filled with peace, harmony, and balance.

257.
I trust in my ability to create a life that is full of purpose and meaning.

258.
I am surrounded by an abundance of positive energy, vibrations, and frequencies.

259.
I let go of any fear, anxiety, or worry.

260.
I am grateful for the strength and resilience of my mind, body, and spirit.

261.
I am open to receiving new opportunities for growth, expansion, and abundance.

262.
I am capable of creating a life filled with joy, positivity, and optimism.

263.
I deserve a life filled with love, compassion, and understanding.

264.
I trust in my ability to create a life that is authentic, genuine, and real.

265.
I am surrounded by an abundance of motivation, inspiration, and encouragement.

266.
I embrace my unique journey and path in life.

267.
I am grateful for the opportunities and blessings that come my way.

268.
I am open to receiving new insights, ideas, and revelations.

269.
I am capable of building a life filled with success, achievement, and accomplishment.

270.
I deserve a life filled with happiness, contentment, and satisfaction.

271.
I trust in my ability to create a life that is rich in love, laughter, and joy.

272.
I am surrounded by an abundance of positivity, enthusiasm, and excitement.

273.
I let go of any self-limiting beliefs or thoughts.

274.
I am grateful for the love and appreciation I have for my body and mind.

275.
I am open to receiving new opportunities for self-discovery and personal growth.

276.
I am capable of creating a life filled with passion, purpose, and meaning.

277.
I deserve a life filled with abundance, prosperity, and wealth.

278.
I trust in my ability to create a life that aligns with my values and beliefs.

279.
I am surrounded by an abundance of creativity, innovation, and inspiration.

280.
I embrace my unique talents, skills, and abilities.

281.
I am grateful for the positive relationships and connections in my life.

282.
I am open to receiving new opportunities for love, romance, and intimacy.

283.
I am capable of building a life filled with success, prosperity, and abundance.

284.
I deserve a life filled with joy, peace, and happiness.

285.
I trust in my ability to create a life that is meaningful, fulfilling, and rewarding.

286.
I am surrounded by an abundance of love, light, and positivity.

287.

I let go of any negative thoughts, emotions, or beliefs.

288.
I am grateful for the strength, courage, and resilience I possess.

289.
I am open to receiving new opportunities for healing, growth, and transformation.

290.
I am capable of creating a life filled with purpose, passion, and joy.

291.
I deserve a life filled with love, happiness, and fulfillment.

292.
I trust in my ability to create a life that is rich in love, laughter, and happiness.

293.
I am surrounded by an abundance of peace, calm, and tranquility.

294.
I embrace my natural beauty and radiance.

295.
I am grateful for the wisdom and knowledge I possess.

296.
I am open to receiving recognition and praise for my accomplishments.

297.
I am capable of creating a life filled with adventure and exploration.

298.

I deserve a strong, healthy body that carries me through life.

299.
I trust in my ability to attract positive people and experiences.

300.
I am surrounded by an abundance of love and support.

301.
I embrace my sensuality and sexual energy.

302.
I am grateful for the courage and bravery I possess.

303.
I am open to receiving new opportunities for growth and expansion.

304.
I am capable of creating a life filled with freedom and flexibility.

305.
I deserve respect, admiration, and appreciation.

306.
I trust in my ability to communicate my thoughts and ideas effectively.

307.
I am surrounded by beauty, wonder, and miracles.

308.
I let go of any fear or worry about the future.

309.
I am grateful for the peace and calm I am able to cultivate within.

310.
I am open to receiving new opportunities for adventure and exploration.

311.
I am capable of building a life filled with joy, ease, and flow.

312.
I deserve a life that exceeds my wildest dreams.

313.
I trust in my ability to handle anything that comes my way.

314.
I am surrounded by positive, supportive, and uplifting people.

315.
I embrace my quirks, flaws, and imperfections.

316.
I am grateful for the abundance and prosperity I experience.

317.
I am open to receiving new opportunities for passion, purpose, and joy.

318.
I am capable of creating a life filled with deep, meaningful connections.

319.
I deserve positive, healthy choices for myself.

320.
I trust in my ability to create an abundance of love, joy, and positivity.

321.
I am surrounded by opportunities for growth, learning, and development.

322.
I let go of any negative self-talk or criticism.

323.
I am grateful for the strength and resilience I have developed.

324.
I am open to receiving guidance and support from my intuition.

325.
I am capable of building a successful, thriving career.

326.
I deserve a life filled with abundance, prosperity, and wealth.

327.
I trust in my ability to create a life that aligns with my values and beliefs.

328.
I am surrounded by an abundance of happiness, laughter, and joy.

329.
I embrace my unique personality and quirks.

330.
I am grateful for the love and appreciation I have for myself.

331.
I am open to receiving new ideas and perspectives.

332.

I am capable of creating a life filled with harmony, balance, and peace.

333.
I deserve a life filled with excitement, adventure, and fun.

334.
I trust in my ability to overcome any challenge or obstacle.

335.
I am surrounded by an abundance of creativity, inspiration, and innovation.

336.
I let go of any limiting beliefs or self-doubt.

337.
I am grateful for the positive impact I have on those around me.

338.
I am open to receiving love, support, and encouragement from others.

339.
I am capable of building a life filled with purpose, meaning, and fulfillment.

340.
I deserve a life filled with passion, romance, and intimacy.

341.
I trust in my ability to create a life that brings me joy and satisfaction.

342.
I am surrounded by an abundance of peace, calm, and tranquility.

343.
I embrace my divine feminine energy and power.

344.
I am grateful for the courage and confidence I possess.

345.
I am open to receiving new opportunities for success and achievement.

346.
I am capable of creating a life filled with love, compassion, and kindness.

347.
I deserve a life filled with joy, happiness, and positivity.

348.
I trust in my ability to create a life that is authentic and true to myself.

349.
I am surrounded by an abundance of motivation, inspiration, and encouragement.

350.
I let go of any past mistakes, regrets, or failures.

351.
I am grateful for the wisdom and knowledge I have gained through my experiences.

352.
I am open to receiving new opportunities for healing and transformation.

353.
I am capable of building a life filled with grace, ease, and flow.

354.

I deserve a life filled with beauty, wonder, and magic.

355.
I trust in my ability to create a life that is rich, fulfilling, and rewarding.

356.
I am surrounded by an abundance of opportunities, possibilities, and potential.

357.
I embrace my unique gifts, talents, and abilities.

358.
I am grateful for the love and support I receive from the universe.

359.
I am open to receiving new opportunities for love, joy, and happiness.

360.
I am capable of creating a life filled with abundance, prosperity, and success.

361.
I deserve a life filled with peace, harmony, and balance.

362.
I trust in my ability to create a life that is full of purpose and meaning.

363.
I am surrounded by an abundance of positive energy, vibrations, and frequencies.

364.
I let go of any fear, anxiety, or worry.

365.
I am grateful for the strength and resilience of my mind, body, and spirit.

366.
I am open to receiving new opportunities for growth, expansion, and abundance.

367.
I am capable of creating a life filled with joy, positivity, and optimism.

368.
I deserve a life filled with love, compassion, and understanding.

369.
I am committed to living a life that is true to my values and beliefs.

370.
I am uplifted by the encouragement and inspiration all around me.

371.
I embrace my unique journey and path in life.

372.
I am grateful for the opportunities and blessings that come my way.

373.
I am open to receiving new insights, ideas, and revelations.

374.
I am capable of building a life filled with success, achievement, and accomplishment.

375.
I deserve a life filled with happiness, contentment, and satisfaction.

376.
I trust in my ability to create a life that is rich in love, laughter, and joy.

377.
I am surrounded by an abundance of positivity, enthusiasm, and excitement.

378.
I let go of any self-limiting beliefs or thoughts.

379.
I am grateful for the love and appreciation I have for my body and mind.

380.
I am open to receiving new opportunities for self-discovery and personal growth.

381.
I am capable of creating a life filled with passion, purpose, and meaning.

382.
I deserve a life filled with abundance, prosperity, and wealth.

383.
I trust in my ability to create a life that aligns with my values and beliefs.

384.
I am surrounded by an abundance of creativity, innovation, and inspiration.

385.
I embrace my unique talents, skills, and abilities.

386.
I am grateful for the positive relationships and connections in my life.

387.
I am open to receiving new opportunities for love, romance, and intimacy.

388.
I am capable of building a life filled with success, prosperity, and abundance.

389.
I deserve a life filled with joy, peace, and happiness.

390.
I trust in my ability to create a life that is meaningful, fulfilling, and rewarding.

391.
I am surrounded by an abundance of love, light, and positivity.

392.
I let go of any negative thoughts, emotions, or beliefs.

393.
I am grateful for the strength, courage, and resilience I possess.

394.
I am open to receiving new opportunities for healing, growth, and transformation.

395.
I am capable of creating a life filled with purpose, passion, and joy.

396.
I deserve a life filled with love, happiness, and fulfillment.

397.
I trust in my ability to create a life that is rich in love, laughter, and happiness.

398.
I am surrounded by an abundance of peace, calm, and tranquility.

399.
I embrace my natural beauty and radiance.

400.
I am grateful for the wisdom and knowledge I possess.

401.
I am open to receiving recognition and praise for my accomplishments.

402.
I am capable of creating a life filled with adventure and exploration.

403.
I deserve a strong, healthy body that carries me through life.

404.
I trust in my ability to attract positive people and experiences.

405.
I am surrounded by an abundance of love and support.

406.
I embrace my sensuality and sexual energy.

407.
I am grateful for the courage and bravery I possess.

408.

I am open to receiving new opportunities for growth and expansion.

409.
I am capable of creating a life filled with freedom and flexibility.

410.
I deserve respect, admiration, and appreciation.

411.
I trust in my ability to communicate my thoughts and ideas effectively.

412.
I am surrounded by beauty, wonder, and miracles.

413.
I let go of any fear or worry about the future.

414.
I am grateful for the peace and calm I am able to cultivate within.

415.
I am open to receiving new opportunities for adventure and exploration.

416.
I am capable of building a life filled with joy, ease, and flow.

417.
I deserve a life that exceeds my wildest dreams.

418.
I trust in my ability to handle anything that comes my way.

419.
I am surrounded by positive, supportive, and uplifting people.

420.
I embrace my quirks, flaws, and imperfections.

421.
I am grateful for the abundance and prosperity I experience.

422.
I am open to receiving new opportunities for passion, purpose, and joy.

423.
I am capable of creating a life filled with deep, meaningful connections.

424.
I deserve positive, healthy choices for myself.

425.
I trust in my ability to create an abundance of love, joy, and positivity.

426.
I am surrounded by opportunities for growth, learning, and development.

427.
I let go of any negative self-talk or criticism.

428.
I am grateful for the strength and resilience I have developed.

429.
I am open to receiving guidance and support from my intuition.

430.
I am capable of building a successful, thriving career.

431.
I deserve a life filled with abundance, prosperity, and wealth.

432.
I trust in my ability to create a life that aligns with my values and beliefs.

433.
I am surrounded by an abundance of happiness, laughter, and joy.

434.
I embrace my unique personality and quirks.

435.
I am grateful for the love and appreciation I have for myself.

436.
I am open to receiving new ideas and perspectives.

437.
I am capable of creating a life filled with harmony, balance, and peace.

438.
I deserve a life filled with excitement, adventure, and fun.

439.
I trust in my ability to overcome any challenge or obstacle.

440.
I am surrounded by an abundance of creativity, inspiration, and innovation.

441.
I let go of any limiting beliefs or self-doubt.

442.

I am grateful for the positive impact I have on those around me.

443.
I am open to receiving love, support, and encouragement from others.

444.
I am capable of building a life filled with purpose, meaning, and fulfillment.

445.
I deserve a life filled with passion, romance, and intimacy.

446.
I trust in my ability to create a life that brings me joy and satisfaction.

447.
I am surrounded by an abundance of peace, calm, and tranquility.

448.
I embrace my divine feminine energy and power.

449.
I am grateful for the courage and confidence I possess.

450.
I am open to receiving new opportunities for success and achievement.

451.
I am capable of creating a life filled with love, compassion, and kindness.

452.
I deserve a life filled with joy, happiness, and positivity.

453.

I trust in my ability to create a life that is authentic and true to myself.

454.
I am surrounded by an abundance of motivation, inspiration, and encouragement.

455.
I let go of any past mistakes, regrets, or failures.

456.
I am grateful for the wisdom and knowledge I have gained through my experiences.

457.
I am open to receiving new opportunities for healing and transformation.

458.
I am capable of building a life filled with grace, ease, and flow.

459.
I deserve a life filled with beauty, wonder, and magic.

460.
I trust in my ability to create a life that is rich, fulfilling, and rewarding.

461.
I am surrounded by an abundance of opportunities, possibilities, and potential.

462.
I embrace my unique gifts, talents, and abilities.

463.
I am grateful for the love and support I receive from the universe.

464.
I am open to receiving new opportunities for love, joy, and happiness.

465.
I am capable of creating a life filled with abundance, prosperity, and success.

466.
I deserve a life filled with peace, harmony, and balance.

467.
I trust in my ability to create a life that is full of purpose and meaning.

468.
I am surrounded by an abundance of positive energy, vibrations, and frequencies.

469.
I let go of any fear, anxiety, or worry.

470.
I am grateful for the strength and resilience of my mind, body, and spirit.

471.
I am open to receiving new opportunities for growth, expansion, and abundance.

472.
I am capable of creating a life filled with joy, positivity, and optimism.

473.
I deserve a life filled with love, compassion, and understanding.

474.
I trust in my ability to create a life that is authentic, genuine, and real.

475.
I find motivation and inspiration in the beauty of everyday moments.

476.
I embrace my unique journey and path in life.

477.
I am grateful for the opportunities and blessings that come my way.

478.
I am open to receiving new insights, ideas, and revelations.

479.
I am capable of building a life filled with success, achievement, and accomplishment.

480.
I deserve a life filled with happiness, contentment, and satisfaction.

481.
I trust in my ability to create a life that is rich in love, laughter, and joy.

482.
I am surrounded by an abundance of positivity, enthusiasm, and excitement.

483.
I let go of any self-limiting beliefs or thoughts.

484.
I am grateful for the love and appreciation I have for my body and mind.

485.

I am open to receiving new opportunities for self-discovery and personal growth.

486.
I am capable of creating a life filled with passion, purpose, and meaning.

487.
I deserve a life filled with abundance, prosperity, and wealth.

488.
I trust in my ability to create a life that aligns with my values and beliefs.

489.
I am surrounded by an abundance of creativity, innovation, and inspiration.

490.
I embrace my unique talents, skills, and abilities.

491.
I am grateful for the positive relationships and connections in my life.

492.
I am open to receiving new opportunities for love, romance, and intimacy.

493.
I am capable of building a life filled with success, prosperity, and abundance.

494.
I deserve a life filled with joy, peace, and happiness.

495.

I trust in my ability to create a life that is meaningful, fulfilling, and rewarding.

496.
I am surrounded by an abundance of love, light, and positivity.

497.
I let go of any negative thoughts, emotions, or beliefs.

498.
I am grateful for the strength, courage, and resilience I possess.

499.
I am open to receiving new opportunities for healing, growth, and transformation.

500.
I am capable of creating a life filled with purpose, passion, and joy.

THE POWER TO INSPIRE AND UPLIFT

"Surround yourself with only people who are going to lift you higher." - Winfrey.

As you reach this milestone in your journey through "1865 Positive Affirmations for Black Women," I invite you to pause and reflect on the transformative power of the affirmations you've encountered thus far. These carefully crafted statements are more than words on a page; they are a catalyst for profound personal growth and empowerment.

Take a moment to consider how these affirmations have resonated with you and the impact they've had on your mindset and daily life. Have you found yourself approaching challenges with renewed strength and resilience? Have you noticed a shift in your self-perception, embracing your unique beauty and worth?

Your experiences and insights are invaluable, and by sharing them, you have the power to inspire and uplift other black women on their own paths to self-discovery. I encourage you to leave a review of this book, detailing the ways in which these affirmations have touched your life and the positive changes you've witnessed within yourself.

Your voice matters, and your story has the potential to create a ripple effect of empowerment and healing within our community. By leaving a review, you not only express gratitude for the impact this book has had on your life but also contribute to a growing movement of black women claiming their power and celebrating their magic.

Scan the QR code to leave your review:

As you continue your journey through the remaining affirmations, keep an open heart and mind and trust in the unfolding of your path. You are exactly where you are meant to be, and your greatest triumphs lie ahead.

With love and solidarity,

Imani

3

AFFIRMATIONS 501 - 750

"You may encounter many defeats, but you must not be defeated. In fact, it may be necessary to encounter the defeats, so you can know who you are, what you can rise from, how you can still come out of it." - Angelou.

501.
I deserve a life filled with love, happiness, and fulfillment.

502.
I trust in my ability to create a life that is rich in love, laughter, and happiness.

503.
I am surrounded by an abundance of peace, calm, and tranquility.

504.
I embrace my natural beauty and radiance.

505.
I am grateful for the wisdom and knowledge I possess.

506.
I am open to receiving recognition and praise for my accomplishments.

507.
I am capable of creating a life filled with adventure and exploration.

508.
I deserve a strong, healthy body that carries me through life.

509.
I trust in my ability to attract positive people and experiences.

510.
I am surrounded by an abundance of love and support.

511.
I embrace my sensuality and sexual energy.

512.
I am grateful for the courage and bravery I possess.

513.
I am open to receiving new opportunities for growth and expansion.

514.
I am capable of creating a life filled with freedom and flexibility.

515.
I deserve respect, admiration, and appreciation.

516.
I trust in my ability to communicate my thoughts and ideas effectively.

517.

I am surrounded by beauty, wonder, and miracles.

518.
I let go of any fear or worry about the future.

519.
I am grateful for the peace and calm I am able to cultivate within.

520.
I am open to receiving new opportunities for adventure and exploration.

521.
I am capable of building a life filled with joy, ease, and flow.

522.
I deserve a life that exceeds my wildest dreams.

523.
I trust in my ability to handle anything that comes my way.

524.
I am surrounded by positive, supportive, and uplifting people.

525.
I embrace my quirks, flaws, and imperfections.

526.
I am grateful for the abundance and prosperity I experience.

527.
I am open to receiving new opportunities for passion, purpose, and joy.

528.

I am capable of creating a life filled with deep, meaningful connections.

529.
I deserve positive, healthy choices for myself.

530.
I trust in my ability to create an abundance of love, joy, and positivity.

531.
I am surrounded by opportunities for growth, learning, and development.

532.
I let go of any negative self-talk or criticism.

533.
I am grateful for the strength and resilience I have developed.

534.
I am open to receiving guidance and support from my intuition.

535.
I am capable of building a successful, thriving career.

536.
I deserve a life filled with abundance, prosperity, and wealth.

537.
I trust in my ability to create a life that aligns with my values and beliefs.

538.
I am surrounded by an abundance of happiness, laughter, and joy.

539.

I embrace my unique personality and quirks.

540.
I am grateful for the love and appreciation I have for myself.

541.
I am open to receiving new ideas and perspectives.

542.
I am capable of creating a life filled with harmony, balance, and peace.

543.
I deserve a life filled with excitement, adventure, and fun.

544.
I trust in my ability to overcome any challenge or obstacle.

545.
I am surrounded by an abundance of creativity, inspiration, and innovation.

546.
I let go of any limiting beliefs or self-doubt.

547.
I am grateful for the positive impact I have on those around me.

548.
I am open to receiving love, support, and encouragement from others.

549.
I am capable of building a life filled with purpose, meaning, and fulfillment.

550.
I deserve a life filled with passion, romance, and intimacy.

551.
I trust in my ability to create a life that brings me joy and satisfaction.

552.
I am surrounded by an abundance of peace, calm, and tranquility.

553.
I embrace my divine feminine energy and power.

554.
I am grateful for the courage and confidence I possess.

555.
I am open to receiving new opportunities for success and achievement.

556.
I am capable of creating a life filled with love, compassion, and kindness.

557.
I deserve a life filled with joy, happiness, and positivity.

558.
I trust in my ability to create a life that is authentic and true to myself.

559.
I am propelled forward by the positive energy surrounding me.

560.
I let go of any past mistakes, regrets, or failures.

561.
I am grateful for the wisdom and knowledge I have gained through my experiences.

562.
I am open to receiving new opportunities for healing and transformation.

563.
I am capable of building a life filled with grace, ease, and flow.

564.
I deserve a life filled with beauty, wonder, and magic.

565.
I trust in my ability to create a life that is rich, fulfilling, and rewarding.

566.
I am surrounded by an abundance of opportunities, possibilities, and potential.

567.
I embrace my unique gifts, talents, and abilities.

568.
I am grateful for the love and support I receive from the universe.

569.
I am open to receiving new opportunities for love, joy, and happiness.

570.
I am capable of creating a life filled with abundance, prosperity, and success.

571.
I deserve a life filled with peace, harmony, and balance.

572.
I trust in my ability to create a life that is full of purpose and meaning.

573.
I am surrounded by an abundance of positive energy, vibrations, and frequencies.

574.
I let go of any fear, anxiety, or worry.

575.
I am grateful for the strength and resilience of my mind, body, and spirit.

576.
I am open to receiving new opportunities for growth, expansion, and abundance.

577.
I am capable of creating a life filled with joy, positivity, and optimism.

578.
I deserve a life filled with love, compassion, and understanding.

579.
I am aligned with my true purpose and passions.

580.
I am surrounded by an abundance of motivation, inspiration, and encouragement.

581.
I embrace my unique journey and path in life.

582.
I am grateful for the opportunities and blessings that come my way.

583.
I am open to receiving new insights, ideas, and revelations.

584.
I am capable of building a life filled with success, achievement, and accomplishment.

585.
I deserve a life filled with happiness, contentment, and satisfaction.

586.
I trust in my ability to create a life that is rich in love, laughter, and joy.

587.
I am surrounded by an abundance of positivity, enthusiasm, and excitement.

588.
I let go of any self-limiting beliefs or thoughts.

589.
I am grateful for the love and appreciation I have for my body and mind.

590.
I am open to receiving new opportunities for self-discovery and personal growth.

591.
I am capable of creating a life filled with passion, purpose, and meaning.

592.
I deserve a life filled with abundance, prosperity, and wealth.

593.
I trust in my ability to create a life that aligns with my values and beliefs.

594.
I am surrounded by an abundance of creativity, innovation, and inspiration.

595.
I embrace my unique talents, skills, and abilities.

596.
I am grateful for the positive relationships and connections in my life.

597.
I am open to receiving new opportunities for love, romance, and intimacy.

598.
I am capable of building a life filled with success, prosperity, and abundance.

599.
I deserve a life filled with joy, peace, and happiness.

600.
I trust in my ability to create a life that is meaningful, fulfilling, and rewarding.

601.
I am surrounded by an abundance of love, light, and positivity.

602.
I let go of any negative thoughts, emotions, or beliefs.

603.
I am grateful for the strength, courage, and resilience I possess.

604.

I am open to receiving new opportunities for healing, growth, and transformation.

605.
I am capable of creating a life filled with purpose, passion, and joy.

606.
I deserve a life filled with love, happiness, and fulfillment.

607.
I trust in my ability to create a life that is rich in love, laughter, and happiness.

608.
I am surrounded by an abundance of peace, calm, and tranquility.

609.
I embrace my natural beauty and radiance.

610.
I am grateful for the wisdom and knowledge I possess.

611.
I am open to receiving recognition and praise for my accomplishments.

612.
I am capable of creating a life filled with adventure and exploration.

613.
I deserve a strong, healthy body that carries me through life.

614.
I trust in my ability to attract positive people and experiences.

615.

I am surrounded by an abundance of love and support.

616.
I embrace my sensuality and sexual energy.

617.
I am grateful for the courage and bravery I possess.

618.
I am open to receiving new opportunities for growth and expansion.

619.
I am capable of creating a life filled with freedom and flexibility.

620.
I deserve respect, admiration, and appreciation.

621.
I trust in my ability to communicate my thoughts and ideas effectively.

622.
I am surrounded by beauty, wonder, and miracles.

623.
I let go of any fear or worry about the future.

624.
I am grateful for the peace and calm I am able to cultivate within.

625.
I am open to receiving new opportunities for adventure and exploration.

626.
I am capable of building a life filled with joy, ease, and flow.

627.
I deserve a life that exceeds my wildest dreams.

628.
I trust in my ability to handle anything that comes my way.

629.
I am surrounded by positive, supportive, and uplifting people.

630.
I embrace my quirks, flaws, and imperfections.

631.
I am grateful for the abundance and prosperity I experience.

632.
I am open to receiving new opportunities for passion, purpose, and joy.

633.
I am capable of creating a life filled with deep, meaningful connections.

634.
I deserve positive, healthy choices for myself.

635.
I trust in my ability to create an abundance of love, joy, and positivity.

636.
I am surrounded by opportunities for growth, learning, and development.

637.
I let go of any negative self-talk or criticism.

638.
I am grateful for the strength and resilience I have developed.

639.
I am open to receiving guidance and support from my intuition.

640.
I am capable of building a successful, thriving career.

641.
I deserve a life filled with abundance, prosperity, and wealth.

642.
I trust in my ability to create a life that aligns with my values and beliefs.

643.
I am surrounded by an abundance of happiness, laughter, and joy.

644.
I embrace my unique personality and quirks.

645.
I am grateful for the love and appreciation I have for myself.

646.
I am open to receiving new ideas and perspectives.

647.
I am capable of creating a life filled with harmony, balance, and peace.

648.
I deserve a life filled with excitement, adventure, and fun.

649.
I trust in my ability to overcome any challenge or obstacle.

650.
I am surrounded by an abundance of creativity, inspiration, and innovation.

651.
I let go of any limiting beliefs or self-doubt.

652.
I am grateful for the positive impact I have on those around me.

653.
I am open to receiving love, support, and encouragement from others.

654.
I am capable of building a life filled with purpose, meaning, and fulfillment.

655.
I deserve a life filled with passion, romance, and intimacy.

656.
I trust in my ability to create a life that brings me joy and satisfaction.

657.
I am surrounded by an abundance of peace, calm, and tranquility.

658.
I embrace my divine feminine energy and power.

659.
I am grateful for the courage and confidence I possess.

660.
I am open to receiving new opportunities for success and achievement.

661.
I am capable of creating a life filled with love, compassion, and kindness.

662.
I deserve a life filled with joy, happiness, and positivity.

663.
I trust in my ability to create a life that is authentic and true to myself.

664.
I am enveloped by an endless supply of inspiration and motivation.

665.
I let go of any past mistakes, regrets, or failures.

666.
I am grateful for the wisdom and knowledge I have gained through my experiences.

667.
I am open to receiving new opportunities for healing and transformation.

668.
I am capable of building a life filled with grace, ease, and flow.

669.
I deserve a life filled with beauty, wonder, and magic.

670.
I trust in my ability to create a life that is rich, fulfilling, and rewarding.

671.

I am surrounded by an abundance of opportunities, possibilities, and potential.

672.
I embrace my unique gifts, talents, and abilities.

673.
I am grateful for the love and support I receive from the universe.

674.
I am open to receiving new opportunities for love, joy, and happiness.

675.
I am capable of creating a life filled with abundance, prosperity, and success.

676.
I deserve a life filled with peace, harmony, and balance.

677.
I trust in my ability to create a life that is full of purpose and meaning.

678.
I am surrounded by an abundance of positive energy, vibrations, and frequencies.

679.
I let go of any fear, anxiety, or worry.

680.
I am grateful for the strength and resilience of my mind, body, and spirit.

681.
I am open to receiving new opportunities for growth, expansion, and abundance.

682.
I am capable of creating a life filled with joy, positivity, and optimism.

683.
I deserve a life filled with love, compassion, and understanding.

684.
I am unapologetically true to myself and my path.

685.
I am surrounded by an abundance of motivation, inspiration, and encouragement.

686.
I embrace my unique journey and path in life.

687.
I am grateful for the opportunities and blessings that come my way.

688.
I am open to receiving new insights, ideas, and revelations.

689.
I am capable of building a life filled with success, achievement, and accomplishment.

690.
I deserve a life filled with happiness, contentment, and satisfaction.

691.
I trust in my ability to create a life that is rich in love, laughter, and joy.

692.
I am surrounded by an abundance of positivity, enthusiasm, and excitement.

693.

I let go of any self-limiting beliefs or thoughts.

694.

I am grateful for the love and appreciation I have for my body and mind.

695.

I am open to receiving new opportunities for self-discovery and personal growth.

696.

I am capable of creating a life filled with passion, purpose, and meaning.

697.

I deserve a life filled with abundance, prosperity, and wealth.

698.

I trust in my ability to create a life that aligns with my values and beliefs.

699.

I am surrounded by an abundance of creativity, innovation, and inspiration.

700.

I embrace my unique talents, skills, and abilities.

701.

I am grateful for the positive relationships and connections in my life.

702.

I am open to receiving new opportunities for love, romance, and intimacy.

703.
I am capable of building a life filled with success, prosperity, and abundance.

704.
I deserve a life filled with joy, peace, and happiness.

705.
I trust in my ability to create a life that is meaningful, fulfilling, and rewarding.

706.
I am surrounded by an abundance of love, light, and positivity.

707.
I let go of any negative thoughts, emotions, or beliefs.

708.
I am grateful for the strength, courage, and resilience I possess.

709.
I am open to receiving new opportunities for healing, growth, and transformation.

710.
I am capable of creating a life filled with purpose, passion, and joy.

711.
I deserve a life filled with love, happiness, and fulfillment.

712.
I trust in my ability to create a life that is rich in love, laughter, and happiness.

713.
I am surrounded by an abundance of peace, calm, and tranquility.

714.
I embrace my natural beauty and radiance.

715.
I am grateful for the wisdom and knowledge I possess.

716.
I am open to receiving recognition and praise for my accomplishments.

717.
I am capable of creating a life filled with adventure and exploration.

718.
I deserve a strong, healthy body that carries me through life.

719.
I trust in my ability to attract positive people and experiences.

720.
I am surrounded by an abundance of love and support.

721.
I embrace my sensuality and sexual energy.

722.
I am grateful for the courage and bravery I possess.

723.
I am open to receiving new opportunities for growth and expansion.

724.
I am capable of creating a life filled with freedom and flexibility.

725.
I deserve respect, admiration, and appreciation.

726.
I trust in my ability to communicate my thoughts and ideas effectively.

727.
I am surrounded by beauty, wonder, and miracles.

728.
I let go of any fear or worry about the future.

729.
I am grateful for the peace and calm I am able to cultivate within.

730.
I am open to receiving new opportunities for adventure and exploration.

731.
I am capable of building a life filled with joy, ease, and flow.

732.
I deserve a life that exceeds my wildest dreams.

733.
I trust in my ability to handle anything that comes my way.

734.
I am surrounded by positive, supportive, and uplifting people.

735.
I embrace my quirks, flaws, and imperfections.

736.
I am grateful for the abundance and prosperity I experience.

737.

I am open to receiving new opportunities for passion, purpose, and joy.

738.
am capable of creating a life filled with deep, meaningful connections.

739.
I deserve positive, healthy choices for myself.

740.
I trust in my ability to create an abundance of love, joy, and positivity.

741.
I am surrounded by opportunities for growth, learning, and development.

742.
I let go of any negative self-talk or criticism.

743.
I am grateful for the strength and resilience I have developed.

744.
I am open to receiving guidance and support from my intuition.

745.
I am capable of building a successful, thriving career.

746.
I deserve a life filled with abundance, prosperity, and wealth.

747.
I trust in my ability to create a life that aligns with my values and beliefs.

748.

I am surrounded by an abundance of happiness, laughter, and joy.

749.
I embrace my unique personality and quirks.

750.
I am grateful for the love and appreciation I have for myself.

4

AFFIRMATIONS 751 - 1001

"The future belongs to those who believe in the beauty of their dreams." — Roosevelt.

751.
I am open to receiving new ideas and perspectives.

752.
I am capable of creating a life filled with harmony, balance, and peace.

753.
I deserve a life filled with excitement, adventure, and fun.

754.
I trust in my ability to overcome any challenge or obstacle.

755.
I am surrounded by an abundance of creativity, inspiration, and innovation.

756.

I let go of any limiting beliefs or self-doubt.

757.
I am grateful for the positive impact I have on those around me.

758.
I am open to receiving love, support, and encouragement from others.

759.
I am capable of building a life filled with purpose, meaning, and fulfillment.

760.
I deserve a life filled with passion, romance, and intimacy.

761.
I trust in my ability to create a life that brings me joy and satisfaction.

762.
I am surrounded by an abundance of peace, calm, and tranquility.

763.
I embrace my divine feminine energy and power.

764.
I am grateful for the courage and confidence I possess.

765.
I am open to receiving new opportunities for success and achievement.

766.
I am capable of creating a life filled with love, compassion, and kindness.

767.

I deserve a life filled with joy, happiness, and positivity.

768.
I trust in my ability to create a life that is authentic and true to myself.

769.
I draw strength from the encouragement and support of others.

770.
I let go of any past mistakes, regrets, or failures.

771.
I am grateful for the wisdom and knowledge I have gained through my experiences.

772.
I am open to receiving new opportunities for healing and transformation.

773.
I am capable of building a life filled with grace, ease, and flow.

774.
I deserve a life filled with beauty, wonder, and magic.

775.
I trust in my ability to create a life that is rich, fulfilling, and rewarding.

776.
I am surrounded by an abundance of opportunities, possibilities, and potential.

777.
I embrace my unique gifts, talents, and abilities.

778.
I am grateful for the love and support I receive from the universe.

779.
I am open to receiving new opportunities for love, joy, and happiness.

780.
I am capable of creating a life filled with abundance, prosperity, and success.

781.
I deserve a life filled with peace, harmony, and balance.

782.
I trust in my ability to create a life that is full of purpose and meaning.

783.
I am surrounded by an abundance of positive energy, vibrations, and frequencies.

784.
I let go of any fear, anxiety, or worry.

785.
I am grateful for the strength and resilience of my mind, body, and spirit.

786.
I am open to receiving new opportunities for growth, expansion, and abundance.

787.
I am capable of creating a life filled with joy, positivity, and optimism.

788.
I deserve a life filled with love, compassion, and understanding.

789.
I am boldly embracing my unique truth and letting it guide me.

790.
I am surrounded by an abundance of motivation, inspiration, and encouragement.

791.
I embrace my unique journey and path in life.

792.
I am grateful for the opportunities and blessings that come my way.

793.
I am open to receiving new insights, ideas, and revelations.

794.
I am capable of building a life filled with success, achievement, and accomplishment.

795.
I deserve a life filled with happiness, contentment, and satisfaction.

796.
I trust in my ability to create a life that is rich in love, laughter, and joy.

797.
I am surrounded by an abundance of positivity, enthusiasm, and excitement.

798.
I let go of any self-limiting beliefs or thoughts.

799.

I am grateful for the love and appreciation I have for my body and mind.

800.
I am open to receiving new opportunities for self-discovery and personal growth.

801.
I am capable of creating a life filled with passion, purpose, and meaning.

802.
I deserve a life filled with abundance, prosperity, and wealth.

803.
I trust in my ability to create a life that aligns with my values and beliefs.

804.
I am surrounded by an abundance of creativity, innovation, and inspiration.

805.
I embrace my unique talents, skills, and abilities.

806.
I am grateful for the positive relationships and connections in my life.

807.
I am open to receiving new opportunities for love, romance, and intimacy.

808.
I am capable of building a life filled with success, prosperity, and abundance.

809.
I deserve a life filled with joy, peace, and happiness.

810.
I trust in my ability to create a life that is meaningful, fulfilling, and rewarding.

811.
I am surrounded by an abundance of love, light, and positivity.

812.
I let go of any negative thoughts, emotions, or beliefs.

813.
I am grateful for the strength, courage, and resilience I possess.

814.
I am open to receiving new opportunities for healing, growth, and transformation.

815.
I am capable of creating a life filled with purpose, passion, and joy.

816.
I deserve a life filled with love, happiness, and fulfillment.

817.
I trust in my ability to create a life that is rich in love, laughter, and happiness.

818.
I am surrounded by an abundance of peace, calm, and tranquility.

819.
I embrace my natural beauty and radiance.

820.
I am grateful for the wisdom and knowledge I possess.

821.
I am open to receiving recognition and praise for my accomplishments.

822.
I am capable of creating a life filled with adventure and exploration.

823.
I deserve a strong, healthy body that carries me through life.

824.
I trust in my ability to attract positive people and experiences.

825.
I am surrounded by an abundance of love and support.

826.
I embrace my sensuality and sexual energy.

827.
I am grateful for the courage and bravery I possess.

828.
I am open to receiving new opportunities for growth and expansion.

829.
I am capable of creating a life filled with freedom and flexibility.

830.
I deserve respect, admiration, and appreciation.

831.

I trust in my ability to communicate my thoughts and ideas effectively.

832.
I am surrounded by beauty, wonder, and miracles.

833.
I let go of any fear or worry about the future.

834.
I am grateful for the peace and calm I am able to cultivate within.

835.
I am open to receiving new opportunities for adventure and exploration.

836.
I am capable of building a life filled with joy, ease, and flow.

837.
I deserve a life that exceeds my wildest dreams.

838.
I trust in my ability to handle anything that comes my way.

839.
I am surrounded by positive, supportive, and uplifting people.

840.
I embrace my quirks, flaws, and imperfections.

841.
I am grateful for the abundance and prosperity I experience.

842.

I am open to receiving new opportunities for passion, purpose, and joy.

843.
I am capable of creating a life filled with deep, meaningful connections.

844.
I deserve positive, healthy choices for myself.

845.
I trust in my ability to create an abundance of love, joy, and positivity.

846.
I am surrounded by opportunities for growth, learning, and development.

847.
I let go of any negative self-talk or criticism.

848.
I am grateful for the strength and resilience I have developed.

849.
I am open to receiving guidance and support from my intuition.

850.
I am capable of building a successful, thriving career.

851.
I deserve a life filled with abundance, prosperity, and wealth.

852.
I trust in my ability to create a life that aligns with my values and beliefs.

853.
I am surrounded by an abundance of happiness, laughter, and joy.

854.
I embrace my unique personality and quirks.

855.
I am grateful for the love and appreciation I have for myself.

856.
I am open to receiving new ideas and perspectives.

857.
I am capable of creating a life filled with harmony, balance, and peace.

858.
I deserve a life filled with excitement, adventure, and fun.

859.
I trust in my ability to overcome any challenge or obstacle.

860.
I am surrounded by an abundance of creativity, inspiration, and innovation.

861.
I let go of any limiting beliefs or self-doubt.

862.
I am grateful for the positive impact I have on those around me.

863.
I am open to receiving love, support, and encouragement from others.

864.

I am capable of building a life filled with purpose, meaning, and fulfillment.

865.
I deserve a life filled with passion, romance, and intimacy.

866.
I trust in my ability to create a life that brings me joy and satisfaction.

867.
I am surrounded by an abundance of peace, calm, and tranquility.

868.
I embrace my divine feminine energy and power.

869.
I am grateful for the courage and confidence I possess.

870.
I am open to receiving new opportunities for success and achievement.

871.
I am capable of creating a life filled with love, compassion, and kindness.

872.
I deserve a life filled with joy, happiness, and positivity.

873.
I trust in my ability to create a life that is authentic and true to myself.

874.
I am inspired by the triumphs and resilience of those who came before me.

875.
I let go of any past mistakes, regrets, or failures.

876.
I am grateful for the wisdom and knowledge I have gained through my experiences.

877.
I am open to receiving new opportunities for healing and transformation.

878.
I am capable of building a life filled with grace, ease, and flow.

879.
I deserve a life filled with beauty, wonder, and magic.

880.
I trust in my ability to create a life that is rich, fulfilling, and rewarding.

881.
I am surrounded by an abundance of opportunities, possibilities, and potential.

882.
I embrace my unique gifts, talents, and abilities.

883.
I am grateful for the love and support I receive from the universe.

884.
I am open to receiving new opportunities for love, joy, and happiness.

885.

I am capable of creating a life filled with abundance, prosperity, and success.

886.
I deserve a life filled with peace, harmony, and balance.

887.
I trust in my ability to create a life that is full of purpose and meaning.

888.
I am surrounded by an abundance of positive energy, vibrations, and frequencies.

889.
I let go of any fear, anxiety, or worry.

890.
I am grateful for the strength and resilience of my mind, body, and spirit.

891.
I am open to receiving new opportunities for growth, expansion, and abundance.

892.
I am capable of creating a life filled with joy, positivity, and optimism.

893.
I deserve a life filled with love, compassion, and understanding.

894.
I am living a genuine life that feels right in my heart.

895.
I am surrounded by an abundance of motivation, inspiration, and encouragement.

896.
I embrace my unique journey and path in life.

897.
I am grateful for the opportunities and blessings that come my way.

898.
I am open to receiving new insights, ideas, and revelations.

899.
I am capable of building a life filled with success, achievement, and accomplishment.

900.
I deserve a life filled with happiness, contentment, and satisfaction.

901.
I trust in my ability to create a life that is rich in love, laughter, and joy.

902.
I am surrounded by an abundance of positivity, enthusiasm, and excitement.

903.
I let go of any self-limiting beliefs or thoughts.

904.
I am grateful for the love and appreciation I have for my body and mind.

905.
I am open to receiving new opportunities for self-discovery and personal growth.

906.

I am capable of creating a life filled with passion, purpose, and meaning.

907.
I deserve a life filled with abundance, prosperity, and wealth.

908.
I trust in my ability to create a life that aligns with my values and beliefs.

909.
I am surrounded by an abundance of creativity, innovation, and inspiration.

910.
I embrace my unique talents, skills, and abilities.

911.
I am grateful for the positive relationships and connections in my life.

912.
I am open to recciving new opportunities for love, romance, and intimacy.

913.
I am capable of building a life filled with success, prosperity, and abundance.

914.
I deserve a life filled with joy, peace, and happiness.

915.
I trust in my ability to create a life that is meaningful, fulfilling, and rewarding.

916.

I am surrounded by an abundance of love, light, and positivity.

917.
I let go of any negative thoughts, emotions, or beliefs.

918.
I am grateful for the strength, courage, and resilience I possess.

919.
I am open to receiving new opportunities for healing, growth, and transformation.

920.
I am capable of creating a life filled with purpose, passion, and joy.

921.
I deserve a life filled with love, happiness, and fulfillment.

922.
I trust in my ability to create a life that is rich in love, laughter, and happiness.

923.
I am surrounded by an abundance of peace, calm, and tranquility.

924.
I embrace my natural beauty and radiance.

925.
I am grateful for the wisdom and knowledge I possess.

926.
I am open to receiving recognition and praise for my accomplishments.

927.

I am capable of creating a life filled with adventure and exploration.

928.
I deserve a strong, healthy body that carries me through life.

929.
I trust in my ability to attract positive people and experiences.

930.
I am surrounded by an abundance of love and support.

931.
I embrace my sensuality and sexual energy.

932.
I am grateful for the courage and bravery I possess.

933.
I am open to receiving new opportunities for growth and expansion.

934.
I am capable of creating a life filled with freedom and flexibility.

935.
I deserve respect, admiration, and appreciation.

936.
I trust in my ability to communicate my thoughts and ideas effectively.

937.
I am surrounded by beauty, wonder, and miracles.

938.
I let go of any fear or worry about the future.

939.

I am grateful for the peace and calm I am able to cultivate within.

940.

I am open to receiving new opportunities for adventure and exploration.

941.

I am capable of building a life filled with joy, ease, and flow.

942.

I deserve a life that exceeds my wildest dreams.

943.

I trust in my ability to handle anything that comes my way.

944.

I am surrounded by positive, supportive, and uplifting people.

945.

I embrace my quirks, flaws, and imperfections.

946.

I am grateful for the abundance and prosperity I experience.

947.

I am open to receiving new opportunities for passion, purpose, and joy.

948.

I am capable of creating a life filled with deep, meaningful connections.

949.

I deserve positive, healthy choices for myself.

950.
I trust in my ability to create an abundance of love, joy, and positivity.

951.
I am surrounded by opportunities for growth, learning, and development.

952.
I let go of any negative self-talk or criticism.

953.
I am grateful for the strength and resilience I have developed.

954.
I am open to receiving guidance and support from my intuition.

955.
I am capable of building a successful, thriving career.

956.
I deserve a life filled with abundance, prosperity, and wealth.

957.
I trust in my ability to create a life that aligns with my values and beliefs.

958.
I am surrounded by an abundance of happiness, laughter, and joy.

959.
I embrace my unique personality and quirks.

960.
I am grateful for the love and appreciation I have for myself.

961.

I am open to receiving new ideas and perspectives.

962.
I am capable of creating a life filled with harmony, balance, and peace.

963.
I deserve a life filled with excitement, adventure, and fun.

964.
I trust in my ability to overcome any challenge or obstacle.

965.
I am surrounded by an abundance of creativity, inspiration, and innovation.

966.
I let go of any limiting beliefs or self-doubt.

967.
I am grateful for the positive impact I have on those around me.

968.
I am open to receiving love, support, and encouragement from others.

969.
I am capable of building a life filled with purpose, meaning, and fulfillment.

970.
I deserve a life filled with passion, romance, and intimacy.

971.
I trust in my ability to create a life that brings me joy and satisfaction.

972.
I am surrounded by an abundance of peace, calm, and tranquility.

973.

I embrace my divine feminine energy and power.

974.

I am grateful for the courage and confidence I possess.

975.

I am open to receiving new opportunities for success and achievement.

976.

I am capable of creating a life filled with love, compassion, and kindness.

977.

I deserve a life filled with joy, happiness, and positivity.

978.

I trust in my ability to create a life that is authentic and true to myself.

979.

I am motivated by the boundless potential within me.

980.

I let go of any past mistakes, regrets, or failures.

981.

I am grateful for the wisdom and knowledge I have gained through my experiences.

982.

I am open to receiving new opportunities for healing and transformation.

983.

I am capable of building a life filled with grace, ease, and flow.

984.
I deserve a life filled with beauty, wonder, and magic.

985.
I trust in my ability to create a life that is rich, fulfilling, and rewarding.

986.
I am surrounded by an abundance of opportunities, possibilities, and potential.

987.
I embrace my unique gifts, talents, and abilities.

988.
I am grateful for the love and support I receive from the universe.

989.
I am open to receiving new opportunities for love, joy, and happiness.

990.
I am capable of creating a life filled with abundance, prosperity, and success.

991.
I deserve a life filled with peace, harmony, and balance.

992.
I trust in my ability to create a life that is full of purpose and meaning.

993.
I am surrounded by an abundance of positive energy, vibrations, and frequencies.

994.
I let go of any fear, anxiety, or worry.

995.

I am grateful for the strength and resilience of my mind, body, and spirit.

996.

I am open to receiving new opportunities for growth, expansion, and abundance.

997.

I am capable of creating a life filled with joy, positivity, and optimism.

998.

I deserve a life filled with love, compassion, and understanding.

999.

I am fearlessly authentic, and my realness inspires others.

1000.

I am surrounded by an abundance of inspiration, guiding me towards my goals.

1001.

I am a powerful, resilient, and magnificent black woman, capable of achieving greatness and living a life filled with purpose, passion, and joy.

CONCLUSION

"Keep your face always toward the sunshine—and shadows will fall behind you." — Whitman

As we come to the end of this transformative journey, I want to remind you of the incredible power and potential that lies within you. Throughout this book, we have explored over 1000 affirmations designed to uplift, empower, and inspire you to create a life that aligns with your deepest desires and values.

Remember, you are the embodiment of strength, resilience, and beauty. You carry within you the wisdom and courage of your ancestors, and you have the power to shape your reality through the thoughts you think and the words you speak.

As you continue on your path, let these affirmations be your guide. Whenever you face challenges or doubts, return to these pages and reconnect with the truth of who you are. You are worthy, deserving, and capable of creating a life filled with abundance, joy, and purpose.

Embrace your unique gifts, celebrate your journey, and trust in the unfolding of your path. You are exactly where you are meant to be, and every experience, whether challenging or joyful, is an opportunity for growth and self-discovery.

Remember to cultivate self-love, self-compassion, and self-acceptance. Treat yourself with the same kindness, understanding, and respect that you would offer to a beloved friend. Nurture your mind, body, and spirit, and surround yourself with people and experiences that uplift and inspire you.

As you move forward, let these affirmations be your daily reminder of the incredible woman you are. Speak them with conviction, feel them in your heart, and watch as your life begins to transform in miraculous ways.

You are a powerful creator, a force for positive change, and a light in this world. Embrace your greatness, trust in your journey, and know that you are capable of achieving anything you set your mind to.

With love, gratitude, and immense respect,

Imani Elkins

THE UNBREAKABLE STRENGTH OF BLACK WOMEN

"The only journey is the one within." — Rilke.

Congratulations on completing this transformative journey through "*1865 Positive Affirmations for Black Women*"! You have taken a courageous step towards embracing your power, cultivating self-love, and redefining your path.

As you close this book, I invite you to reflect on the profound impact these affirmations have had on your life. Have you noticed a shift in your self-talk, replacing negative thoughts with empowering, affirming ones? Have you found yourself approaching challenges with a renewed sense of confidence and resilience? Have you begun to celebrate your unique gifts and unapologetically embrace your greatness?

Your experiences and triumphs are a testament to the transformative power of positive affirmations and the unbreakable strength of black women. By sharing your story, you have the opportunity to inspire and uplift countless others on their own journeys of self-discovery and empowerment.

I urge you to leave a review of this book, detailing the ways in which these affirmations have resonated with you and the positive changes you've experienced as a result. Your words have the power to create a ripple effect of healing, growth, and solidarity within our community.

By leaving a review, you not only express gratitude for the impact this book has had on your life but also contribute to a growing movement of black women claiming their power, celebrating their magic, and redefining their narratives.

Remember, your voice matters, and your story has the potential to change lives. Share your experience, and let your light shine brightly for all to see.

To leave a review, simply scan the QR code:

With immense love, gratitude, and respect,

Imani

BIBLIOGRAPHY

Angelou, M. (1978). And still I rise. Random House.

Blackstone, A. M. (2018). The little book of big affirmations: 365 affirmations for a happy and fulfilling life. Adams Media.

Buddha. (n.d.). You yourself, as much as anybody in the entire universe, deserve your love and affection. Retrieved from https://www.goodreads.com/quotes/263329-you-yourself-as-much-as-anybody-in-the-entire-universe

Hay, L. (1984). You can heal your life. Hay House.

Heinz, A. (2019). The self-love workbook: A life-changing guide to boost self-esteem, recognize your worth and find genuine happiness. Zeitgeist.

Hooks, b. (2000). All about love: New visions. William Morrow Paperbacks.

Morrison, T. (1987). Beloved. Alfred A. Knopf.

National Archives. (2022). 13th Amendment to the U.S. Constitution. https://www.archives.gov/historical-docs/13th-amendment

Nelson, N. (2020). Don't touch my hair! Carolrhoda Books.

Peale, N. V. (1952). The power of positive thinking. Prentice-Hall.

Rilke, R. M. (n.d.). The only journey is the one within. Retrieved from https://www.goodreads.com/quotes/19445-the-only-journey-is-the-one-within

Roosevelt, E. (n.d.). The future belongs to those who believe in the beauty of their dreams. Retrieved from https://www.brainyquote.com/quotes/eleanor_roosevelt_121494

Walker, A. (1983). In search of our mothers' gardens: Womanist prose. Harcourt Brace Jovanovich.

Whitman, W. (n.d.). Keep your face always toward the sunshine—and shadows will fall behind you. Retrieved from https://www.goodreads.com/quotes/75212-keep-your-face-always-toward-the-sunshine---and-shadows-will

Williamson, M. (1992). A return to love: Reflections on the principles of a course in miracles. HarperCollins.

Winfrey, O. (n.d.). Surround yourself with only people who are going to lift you higher. Retrieved from https://www.brainyquote.com/quotes/oprah_winfrey_378295

Ziglar, Z. (n.d.). What you get by achieving your goals is not as important as what you become by achieving your goals. Retrieved from https://www.brainyquote.com/quotes/zig_ziglar_389904

www.ingramcontent.com/pod-product-compliance
Lightning Source LLC
Chambersburg PA
CBHW072053110526
44590CB00018B/3154